DIARY OF THE FALL

A man examines the mistakes of his past, struggling for forgiveness; haunted by the childhood prank that went horribly wrong. His father has started a memoir, obsessed with recording every recollection he can before he loses them to Alzheimer's. And his grandfather, a survivor of Auschwitz, fills notebook after notebook with the false memories of someone desperate to forget . . .

MICHEL LAUB

◆

DIARY OF THE FALL

Translated from the Portuguese by
Margaret Jull Costa

Complete and Unabridged

ULVERSCROFT
Leicester

First published in Great Britain in 2014 by
Harvill Secker
London

First Large Print Edition
published 2015
by arrangement with
Harvill Secker
The Random House Group Limited
London

A catalogue record for this book is available
from the British Library.

ISBN 978–1–4448–2615–9

Published by
F. A. Thorpe (Publishing)
Anstey, Leicestershire

Set by Words & Graphics Ltd.
Anstey, Leicestershire
Printed and bound in Great Britain by
T. J. International Ltd., Padstow, Cornwall

This book is printed on acid-free paper

For my father

A FEW THINGS I KNOW ABOUT MY GRANDFATHER

1.

My grandfather didn't like to talk about the past, which is not so very surprising given its nature: the fact that he was a Jew, had arrived in Brazil on one of those jam-packed ships, as one of the cattle for whom history appears to have ended when they were twenty, or thirty, or forty or whatever, and for whom all that's left is a kind of memory that comes and goes and that can turn out to be an even worse prison than the one they were in.

2.

In my grandfather's notebooks, there is no mention of that journey at all. I don't know where he boarded the ship, if he managed to get some sort of documentation before he left, if he had any money or at least an inkling of what awaited him in Brazil. I don't know how long the crossing lasted, whether it was windy or calm, whether they were struck by a storm one night in the early hours, whether he even cared if the ship went down and he died in what would seem a highly ironic manner, in a dark whirlpool of ice and with no hope of being remembered by anyone except as a statistic — a fact that would sum up his entire biography, swallowing up any reference to the place where he had spent his childhood and the school where he studied and everything else that had happened in his life in the interval between being born and the day he had a number tattooed on his arm.

3.

I don't want to talk about it either. If there's one thing the world doesn't need it's to hear my thoughts on the subject. It's been dealt with in the cinema. It's been dealt with in books. Eyewitnesses have already recounted the story detail by detail, and there are sixty years of reports and essays and analyses, generations of historians and philosophers and artists who devoted their lives to adding footnotes to all that material in an effort to refresh yet again the world's views on the matter, the reflex reaction everyone has to the word *Auschwitz*, so not for a second would it occur to me to repeat those ideas if they were not, in some way, essential if I am to talk about my grandfather and, therefore, about my father and, therefore, about myself.

4.

In the months prior to my thirteenth birthday I was studying to prepare for my bar mitzvah. Twice a week I went to the house of a rabbi. There were six or seven of us in the class, and we each took home with us a tape on which he had recorded extracts from the Torah sung by him. By the next class we were expected to know the whole thing by heart, and even today I can still sing that fifteen- or twenty-minute mantra without understanding a single word.

5.

The rabbi lived on his salary from the synagogue and on contributions from the families who attended. His wife had died and he had no children. During class he drank tea with sweetener in it. Shortly after the class began, he would pick on one of the students, usually the one who hadn't done his homework, sit down beside him, speak to him with his face almost pressed to his, and make him sing each line and syllable over and over, until the student got it wrong for the second or third time, then the rabbi would thump the table and shout and say that he wouldn't bar-mitzvah any of us.

6.

The rabbi had long fingernails and smelled of vinegar. He was the only rabbi in the city who gave those preparatory classes. After the class, we would often have to wait in the kitchen while he talked to our parents, telling them how indifferent, undisciplined, ignorant and aggressive we were, and after this speech he would always ask them for a little more money. It often happened, too, that one of the students, knowing the rabbi had diabetes and had already spent time in hospital, where, due to complications, he had almost ended up having one of his legs amputated, that this student would offer to make him another cup of tea, adding sugar this time instead of sweetener.

7.

Almost all my schoolfriends were barmitzvahed. The ceremony always took place on a Saturday morning. The birthday boy would wear the tallit and be called upon to pray along with the adults. Then there would be a lunch or a dinner, usually held in some posh hotel, and one of my schoolfriends' favourite tricks was to put shoe polish on the door handles of the rooms. Another favourite trick was to pee in the boxes of hand towels provided in the gentlemen's toilets. There was another trick too, although it only happened once, when it was time to sing 'Happy Birthday', and because that particular year it had become the custom to give the birthday boy the bumps, tossing him into the air thirteen times, with a group of boys catching him as he fell, like a fireman's safety net — except that on the day in question the net disappeared on the thirteenth fall and the birthday boy crashed to the floor.

8.

The party where this happened wasn't held at a posh hotel, but in the reception room of a building without a lift or a porter, because the birthday boy was also a scholarship boy and the son of a bus conductor, who had once been spotted selling candyfloss in the park. The birthday boy had never had to resit a single subject, had never been to any parties, never been involved in a riot in the library, nor was he among the students who put a slab of raw meat in a female teacher's handbag, and he certainly wasn't amused when someone left a bomb behind the toilets, a bag of gunpowder attached to a lit cigar. When he fell he bruised a vertebra, had to stay in bed for two months, wear an orthopaedic corset for a further few months and go to a physiotherapist during the whole of that time, on top of being taken to hospital and having his party end in a general atmosphere of perplexity, at least among the adults present — and one of the boys who should have caught him was me.

9.

A Jewish school, at least a school like ours, in which some students are dropped off in a chauffeur-driven car and others spend years being ridiculed, one of them having his packed lunch spat in every day, another being locked in the machine room during every break-time, and the student who was injured during his birthday party had already been the victim of such pranks, having in previous years been repeatedly buried in the sand

— yes, a Jewish school is much like any other. The difference being that you spend your childhood being told about anti-Semitism: some teachers talk of little else, as a way of explaining the atrocities committed by the Nazis, which were a consequence of the atrocities committed by the Poles, which were an echo of the atrocities committed by the Russians, and you could add to this list the Arabs, the Muslims, the Christians and anyone else you care to name, a spiral of hatred that had its roots in feelings of envy for the intelligence, willpower, culture and wealth that the Jews had created despite all those obstacles.

10.

When I was thirteen, I lived in a house with a swimming pool, and in the summer holidays I went to Disneyland and rode on Space Mountain, saw the Pirates of the Caribbean and the parade and the fireworks, and afterwards visited the Epcot Center and saw the dolphins at Sea World and the crocodiles in Cypress Gardens and the river rapids in Busch Gardens and the vampire mirrors in the Mystery Fun House.

11.

When I was thirteen I had: a video game, a VCR, a shelf full of books and records, a guitar, a pair of roller skates, a NASA uniform, a stolen No Parking sign, a tennis racquet I never used, a tent, a skateboard, a rubber ring, a Rubik's cube, a knuckleduster, and a small penknife.

12.

When I was thirteen I had still never had a girlfriend. I had never been really ill. I had never seen anyone die or have a serious accident. On the night that the birthday boy fell I dreamed about his father, about his aunts and uncles and grandparents, who had all been there, about his godfather, who had perhaps helped pay for the party, even though all they provided was chocolate cake and popcorn and chicken croquettes and paper plates.

13.

I often dreamed about the moment of the fall, a silence that lasted a second, possibly two, a room full of sixty people and no one making a sound, as if everyone were waiting for my classmate to cry out, or even just grunt, but he lay on the ground with his eyes closed until someone told everyone else to move away because he might be injured, a scene that stayed with me until he came back to school and crept along the corridors, wearing his orthopaedic corset underneath his uniform in the cold, the heat, the sun and the rain.

14.

If, at the time, someone had asked me what affected me most deeply, seeing what happened to my classmate or the fact that my grandfather had been imprisoned in Auschwitz, and by 'affect' I mean to experience something intensely as palpable and ever present, a memory that doesn't even need to be evoked to appear, I would have had no hesitation in giving my answer.

15.

My grandfather died when my father was fourteen. The image I have of him comes from half a dozen photographs, in which he is always wearing the same clothes, the same dark suit, the same hair and beard, and I have no idea what his voice sounded like, and I don't even know if his teeth were white because in none of the photos is he smiling.

16.

I never knew my grandfather's house, but some of the furniture from there, the armchair, the round table, the glass cabinet, ended up in the apartment where my grandmother went to live afterwards. It was an apartment better suited to a widow who rarely went out, at most once a week to have tea at a friend's house, a habit she kept up until the friend had to move into an old people's home, where she spent five or ten years, during which time she broke a leg and then her pelvis and suffered at least three bouts of pneumonia, a heart attack and a stroke before she died.

17.

I once visited that home with my grand- mother. It was right on the outskirts of the city. The rooms smelled of eucalyptus, and the building was surrounded by a green area with benches and flower beds, and from there we could see the nurses, the visiting relatives, the occasional uniformed care assistant, and sometimes a gentleman in a motorised wheelchair equipped with an oxygen cylinder. My grandmother and her friend discussed the latest TV soap, the violence reported in the newspapers, how people in the street were growing ever ruder and the cold days ever longer, and at no point in the conversation, nor in any conversation I had with my grandmother until she died, more or less as her friend in the home had done, except without a heart attack along the way, and the stroke she had was so massive that it spared everyone having to see her lying in bed during that eternity in which the person can neither speak nor move — at no point in her life did my grandmother mention my grandfather.

18.

I mean, sometimes she would say very obvious things, that my grandfather didn't talk much, that he slept in long-sleeved pyjamas even in summer, that when they

13

were first married he would do fifteen minutes of exercises when he got up, and that he once fell off the ladder he would use to get into the loft, and I could continue that list until there were twenty items or perhaps even thirty, but at no point in all those years did she tell me the most important thing about him.

19.

In the final years of his life, my grandfather spent the whole day in his study. Only after he died did we find out what he had been doing there, notebooks and more notebooks filled with tiny writing, and only when I read what he had written did I finally understand what he had been through. It was then that his experience stopped being merely histori- cal, merely collective, merely attached to some abstract moral, in the sense that Auschwitz became a kind of landmark in which you believe with all the force of your education, your reading, all the debates you've heard on the subject, the positions you've solemnly defended, the vehemently condemnatory statements you've made with- out for a second feeling as if any of that experience were truly yours.

20.

If I had to speak about something that was truly mine, I would start with the story of that classmate who fell at the party. About how he reappeared at school months later. About how I found the courage to go over to him and speak and ask a question when the two of us were waiting in the corridor for the next class and make some comment regarding the following week's test or the teacher's dandruff-covered jacket, and about the way in which he responded to my comment, as if we were having a perfectly normal conversation and as if either of us could possibly forget that he was wearing an orthopaedic corset, and that whenever he stood up it felt as if everyone were watching to see if he walked any differently, raising one foot higher than the other, a slightly irregular rhythm that would stay with him for ever, as it would with the other boys who were there at that party.

21.

My classmate's name was João, and as we grew closer I learned that: (a) his father sold candyfloss in the park because he didn't earn enough as a bus conductor; (b) his father had brought him up alone because João's mother had died before she was forty; (c) after his mother died, his father never married again or had more children or even a girlfriend.

22.

About João I learned that: (a) he never said anything to his father about getting buried in sand every day; (b) he told him that the reason he never phoned up a friend to go out to play was because he preferred to stay at home studying; (c) he never attributed any of his problems at school to the fact that he wasn't Jewish.

23.

My school had a tradition of getting students into the best universities, the ones that produced industrialists, engineers and lawyers. João's father thought it was worth the sacrifice to enrol João in such a prestigious school, and through the scholarship programme he managed to get an eighty per cent discount on the monthly fees. However, he still had to work really hard to pay the remaining twenty per cent, plus the uniform, books and transport.

24.

João's father decided to celebrate his son's thirteenth birthday because the family had never given a proper party. Aside from birthdays when João was a child, they usually only invited relatives over for a beer, and João didn't normally invite anyone apart from a cousin and a boy from the same building who was four years younger than him. But because João was attending a Jewish school and all the boys there were bar-mitzvahed at the age of thirteen, and at every party the birthday boy was given thirteen bumps, a kind of initiation into the adult world, when, to use the Hebrew expression that gives the ceremony its name, the boy became 'a son of commandment', for all those reasons João's father persuaded his son to invite his classmates to the reception room in the building where one of his brothers-in-law lived.

25.

I only found this out months later, when I was already a regular visitor to their apartment. They lived in an even more modest building than the brother-in-law, a place of peeling walls and bare wires, and when I arrived there one afternoon, quite late in the day, João was out. He had gone to pay a bill or post a letter or take something to the registry office, one of the various errands he ran in order to help out at home, and his father opened the door to me and offered me a glass of fruit juice. We sat down in front of the TV. The local news was on. We sat there for some time, not saying anything, as was perfectly normal, because up until then I had never exchanged more than a few words with him, and when the silence became ever more uncomfortable and the daily soap ever more tedious, and because it was nearly dark and João had still not come back, he started asking me questions — about school, about my father, about my grandfather.

26.

João's father listened to me with the TV still on, and it was as if he wasn't interested in anything I was saying, because he kept looking straight ahead, even occasionally changing channels. At one point, he commented on a game show in which the audience begged for money, the toothless, the blind, the deaf, people covered in sores and burns, and João's father said how absurd to allow those people to appear on TV, how absurd to treat them like that, how absurd that the government did nothing about it. I'm sick of living in this shithole of a country. Don't you agree that this is a shithole of a country? That everything we do turns to shit? That the people in it are nothing but shit? And then he got up, turned off the TV and started talking about himself and his son and about life, and then, with the same anger in his voice, fixing me with his eyes as if he had been waiting for this moment for a very long time, he asked if I didn't feel ashamed about what had happened at João's birthday party.

27.

In a school like mine, the few non-Jewish students even enjoyed certain privileges. For example, they didn't have to attend Hebrew classes. Or the classes about Hebrew culture. In the weeks preceding religious holidays, they were excused from learning the traditional songs, saying the prayers, doing the dances, taking part in the Shabbat, visiting the synagogue and the Old People's Home, and decorating Moses' cradle to the sound of the Israeli national anthem, not to mention the so-called Youth Movement camps.

28.

At camp we were divided into groups, each with an older boy as a monitor, and part of the day was taken up with the usual activities one would expect at such a gathering: lunch, football, group hugs, treasure hunts and messy games involving talcum powder and eggs. We took a tent, insect repellent, a cooking pot and a canteen, and I remember carefully hiding anything that might be stolen in my absence, stowing a bar of chocolate at the bottom of my dirty laundry bag, a battery charger in the middle of a clump of nettles.

29.

At night we were divided into two groups, in an exercise known as 'camp attack', with one group hidden in the vegetation and the other in charge of defending the camp. Then, in a clearing in the early hours, we would form into platoons that basically did what patrols are supposed to do, armed with compasses and in columns, crawling through undergrowth and scaling hills, an imitation of what we had heard about in talks the monitors gave about the Six-Day War, the War of Independence, the Yom Kippur War, the Lebanese War.

30.

There were other non-Jews at the school, but none like João. Once, one of them got hold of a Jewish classmate, dragged him along for about forty metres, pinned his victim's right arm to the wall next to an iron door and repeatedly slammed the door on the boy's fingers, and when the boy was screaming and writhing in pain, he grabbed the boy's left arm and did the same again. João was different: if a classmate ordered him to stand, he would stand. If a classmate flung João's sandwich across the playground, João would go and fetch it. If the same classmate then grabbed João and made him eat the sandwich, bite by bite, João's face would remain utterly impassive — no pain, no pleading, no expression at all.

31

When João's father asked me if I didn't feel ashamed about what had happened at the party, I could have described that scene to him. I could have told him more than he was expecting to hear, rather than about how I had apologised to João when he returned to school. Instead of telling him how relieved I felt when I found out that João would make a full recovery, walking normally and leading a normal life, and how knowing this had made our conversation easier, as if my apology had instantly erased everything he had been through after the fall, João lying on the floor in front of his relatives, the breath knocked out of him, João in the ambulance and at the A&E department and in hospital, where not a single one of his classmates visited him, and then another two months spent at home, where, again, none of us went to see him, and then back at school where, again, none of us spoke to him until I plucked up enough courage to do so — instead of that I could have told him what it was like to see João eating that sandwich watched by his attacker. And how, when he had finished the last mouthful, his attacker had hit him again, hidden behind a tree in one corner of the playground, surrounded by a small group of boys who chanted the same refrain every day.

32.

The refrain went like this: *eat sand, eat sand*. It was a sort of ritual, intended to drive them on while João turned his head to try and avoid the blows, until he could resist no longer and opened his mouth, the hot, rough taste, the sole of someone's trainer in his face, and only then did his attacker grow weary and the shouting diminish and then João would be left to get up on his own, red-faced and straightening his rumpled clothes, picking up his backpack and going up the stairs like a public admission of how dirty and weak and despicable he was.

33.

None of this prevented him from coming to school with the invitations to his party. For bar mitzvah ceremonies, the invitations were always professionally printed on a folded piece of card, with a ribbon and gilt lettering, the name of the boy's parents, a telephone number to confirm that you would be coming and an address where presents could be sent. João's invitations were home-made on a sheet of foolscap paper placed in a cardboard envelope and written in felt-tip pen. Two weeks beforehand, he silently gave them out, going from desk to desk, inviting the whole year group.

34.

That Saturday I woke up early. I got dressed, went to the fridge and spent the morning in my room. I liked watching TV like that, with the blinds down, the bed still unmade and bread-crumbs among the sheets, until someone knocked on the door to tell me it was a quarter to one, and the rest of the day was: lunch at my grandmother's house, a visit to the shopping mall with my mother, her asking me if the classmate whose birthday it was would prefer a pair of shorts or a backpack, a wallet or a T-shirt, or if he liked music and would be happy with a record voucher, and me answering and waiting for her to pay and for the assistant to wrap the present up and then still having time to visit the arcade where I played at circuit racing and electronic snooker.

35.

I wished João a happy birthday when I arrived at the party. I gave him his present. I may have said hello to his father too, or to some relative of his standing nearby, and I may even have enjoyed the party along with all the other guests, I may even have had a good time without for a moment appearing nervous, along with the four other classmates chosen to form the safety net, and who I had also greeted when I arrived, and with whom I chatted normally, all of us dressed and ready and united as we waited for the moment for the birthday cake to be cut and for everyone to sing 'Happy Birthday'.

36.

I don't know if I took part because of those other classmates, and it would be easy at this stage to blame them for everything, or if at some point I played an active role in the story: if during the previous days I had an idea, made a suggestion, and was in some way indispensable if everything was to work out as planned, with us singing the last line together, *happy birthday to you*, before we gathered round him, one at each leg, one at each arm, with me supporting his neck because that's the most vulnerable part of the body.

37.

I don't know if I did it simply because I was mirroring my classmates' behaviour, João being thrown into the air once, twice, with me supporting him right up until the thirteenth time and then, as he was going up, withdrawing my arms and taking a step back and seeing João hover in the air and then begin the fall, or was it the other way round: what if, deep down, because of that plot hatched in the previous days, because of something I might have said or an attitude I might have taken, even if only once and in the presence of only one other person, quite independently of the circumstances and any possible excuses, what if, deep down, they were also mirroring my behaviour?

38.

Because of course I used the same words, the words that led up to the moment when the back of his neck struck the floor, and it didn't take long for me to notice my classmates beating a hasty retreat, just ten steps to the corridor and the porter's lodge and the street and suddenly you're tearing round the corner without a backward glance and not even thinking that if you had only reached out an arm to break the fall João would have got up, and I would never have had to see in him the consequence of everything I had done up until then, school, break-time, the stairs and the playground and the wall where João used to sit, the sandwich flung across the playground and João buried in sand and me allowing myself to be carried along with the others, repeating the same words, the same rhythm, all of us together at the same time, the song you sing because that's all you can do when you're thirteen: *eat sand, eat sand, son-of-a-bitch goy.*

A FEW THINGS I KNOW ABOUT MY FATHER

1.

The first entry in my grandfather's notebooks is about the day he disembarked in Brazil. I've read dozens of accounts written by immigrants, and new arrivals tend to remark upon the heat, the humidity, the uniforms worn by the immigration staff, the army of petty con men who gather at the port, the skin colour of someone sleeping on a pile of sawdust, but my grandfather's first sentence is about a glass of milk.

2.

It seems that my grandfather wanted to write a kind of encyclopedia, an accumulation of apparently unrelated words, each followed by a short or long text, and each with its own peculiar characteristic. The entry for *milk*, for example, speaks of *a liquid food with a creamy texture, which as well as containing calcium and other substances essential to the organism has the advantage of not being highly susceptible to the development of bacteria.*

3.

My grandfather then moves on to *port,
luggage* and *Sesefredo,* and it isn't hard to
see that the words occur in the order in
which he came across each of those places,
objects, people and situations. You can follow
the sequence as if it were a story, but
because the entries are so obviously
contrived and written in such a crassly
optimistic tone, the effect is quite the
opposite: my grandfather writes that there is
no record of any illnesses being caused by
drinking milk, that the port is *the meeting
place for street vendors whose work is
subject to strict fiscal and hygienic controls,*
and it isn't hard to imagine him there on the
quay, having eaten the last slices of the dry
bread that was his only food on the voyage,
and drinking his first glass of milk in years,
the milk of the new world and the new life,
poured from a jug kept who knows where or
how or for how long, and because of which
he would almost die.

4.

The Jewish immigrants who arrived in the
south of Brazil — initially in the port of

Santos, then travelling from there to Rio Grande and finally in a small steamship to Porto Alegre — usually stayed in the homes of relatives or distant acquaintances or in small guesthouses in the centre. The name of the guesthouse where my grandfather stayed was Sesefredo. In the notebooks, he defines it as *a clean spacious establishment, quiet in the mornings and cosy and welcoming when night falls.* A place where someone with typhoid fever, probably contracted from drinking a contaminated glass of milk, is cared for by the generous owners who speak German and explain in German the nature of the illness, its symptoms and the twenty-five per cent mortality rate, and this in an age when the necessary antibiotics had not yet been invented or had not yet reached Brazil or not at least that particular guesthouse. In the Sesefredo Guesthouse it was possible to withstand those four weeks of vomiting, headache, malaise and a forty-degree fever thanks to *the kindness of its owners,* the couple who never threaten their new guest or spend those four weeks saying that they will kick him out into the street as soon as his last centavo has gone.

5.

Unlike my grandmother, my father spoke little about the banal details of my grandfather's life. Perhaps because he died when my father was fourteen, and so what would be the point of wondering if my grandfather used to arrive promptly at work, if he was nice to the customers, if he treated his employees well, if he enjoyed what he did for ten or twelve hours a day until he retired and spent what remained of his life at home, shut up in his study, and if during all that time he made any comment about the house where they lived, the city or the country, about something he had seen or experienced, something that would remove from him the label that was always present in any conversation I had with my father on the subject: the man who survived Nazism, the war, Auschwitz.

6.

My father spoke a great deal about the Germany of the 1930s, about how easily the Jews were deceived, and how easy it was to believe that a raid on a house was an isolated event, that the appearance one morning of a Star of David daubed on the door of an optician's or a hardware store was the work of a group of vandals, because if you own a business and pay your taxes and create employment and feel comfortably at home in the country where three generations of your family have lived, you're not going to want to believe in the possibility that you might lose everything, and from one day to the next have to board a ship, with only the clothes on your back, heading for some place about whose customs, politics or history you know nothing.

7.

In my grandfather's notebooks, the Brazil of 1945 was a country that had never experienced slavery. Where no immigration officers placed restrictions on the arrival of immigrants fleeing the war. A land full of opportunities for a teacher of mathematics who spoke no Portuguese, and so as soon as he had recovered from typhoid, my grandfather began looking for work, which would not be hard given the huge demand in the schools, universities and institutes that made of Porto Alegre a place of scientific excellence, where there were regular symposia on art and philosophy, pleasant events followed by pleasant evenings spent in one of the innumerable cafés in the centre frequented, naturally enough, by *pretty single women*, whose parents would be delighted to be introduced to a Jew.

8.

Imagine a wealthy house in Porto Alegre in 1945. Imagine a dinner party at such a house, the table at one end of the dining room, a family speaking various languages, even or especially German. The family is served by uniformed staff and they pass comment perhaps on the swearing-in of the new President Eurico Gaspar Dutra, who my grandfather has never heard of, or a speech by Carlos Lacerda, who my grandfather has never heard of either, just as he has never heard of any of the other familiar references of the period, the casinos, Rádio Nacional, the showgirls in the cabarets, and, as the evening wears on, people drink and offer toasts and at no point does the owner of the house address my grandfather except to remark that the world would be a worse place now that the Americans had won the war.

9.

There are many ways of knowing how things actually happened. In this case, the story was told to my father by my grandmother. It is, besides, a banal enough story, and for me its sole interest lies in being able to compare it with my grandfather's entry in his notebook: the house he describes is quite different, the owner of the house played records of music by Bach and Schubert and even made a joke about Schubert having died of typhoid fever, which did not strike my grandfather as in the least offensive — on the contrary, it was just a way of breaking the ice when, accompanied by my grandmother, he arrived as that evening's special guest to whom the owner of the house offered a glass of wine, before inviting him to take his place at the table, telling a few more jokes and praising the readiness of Dutra's party to *reaffirm Brazil's natural vocation for democracy*.

10.

According to my grandfather, it was normal in Porto Alegre in 1945 for a rich, Germanophile father with a pretty single daughter, when confronted by a poor Jewish immigrant recently recovered from typhoid fever and owing two months' rent at a guesthouse called Sesefredo, to ask that young man what his intentions were towards his daughter. It was normal for the young man to answer that he would like to resume his career as a teacher, but that, given his difficulties with the Portuguese language, which he would soon overcome, as well as certain expectations on the part of the owners of the Sesefredo Guesthouse, always expressed *in a sympathetic, cordial manner*, he was thinking of taking a temporary job as a travelling salesman offered to him by an agent, and which would require him to travel to sixteen towns a week selling sewing machines. There are various types of machine, the young man explains, with different uses and prices, and then the rich father of the pretty, single daughter smiles broadly and offers him another glass of wine and a cigar too, and at the end of that pleasant supper, they both toast to the fact that the young man will take the daughter of that proud, rich man to live in a one-bedroom apartment near to the Sesefredo Guesthouse, in a street where there are kennels and a poultry slaughterhouse, *commercial establishments of unimpeachable reputation*, in a building that survived a fire, but which is nonetheless *solid and with a pleasant aspect to the sun*, a place in which to start a new life to be commemorated in a ceremony a few months later, with a priest and a rabbi present to celebrate the union of the daughter of that proud, rich man and his poor, Jewish son-in-law, who will soon give him his one grandchild.

11.

When my father was born, it had been two years since my grandmother had spoken to my great-grandfather. She left home telling him that not only did she intend to stay with my grandfather, but that she also intended converting to Judaism. Conversion is not a simple process, because Judaism makes little effort to attract converts, and you have to submit to a long process of reading, living a Jewish life and talking to a rabbi, and on the day of her conversion the woman receives a Hebrew name and is immersed in a ritual bath of rainwater collected for that purpose, and I don't know if my grandmother did this because of my grandfather, so that she could be closer to him, or if it was a reaction to her own family's opposition to the marriage.

12.

My great-grandfather never forgave my grandmother. My great-grandmother stopped talking to her too. My grandmother had an older sister, who married a farmer in the interior of Rio Grande do Sul, and a younger brother who was studying to be a diplomat, and not one of them is alive today: my great-grandfather died from a heart attack, my great-grandmother in a car accident, my grandmother's sister of tuberculosis, her brother from complications following appendicitis.

13.

Everyone on my grandfather's side died in Auschwitz, and there isn't a single line about them in the notebooks. There isn't a line about the camp itself, how long my grandfather spent there, how he managed to survive or what he felt when he was freed, and I can imagine my father's reaction when he read those notebooks six months or a year after my grandfather's death and noticed these omissions.

14.

My grandfather wrote nothing about Judaism. He made no comment about my grandmother's conversion. Nor any account of her attempts to understand the religion after she had converted, the books she read, her visits to the synagogue unaccompanied by him, the questions she asked and to which he gave only the briefest of answers. It's possible that my father never heard him say anything on the subject when he was a child or indeed before the age of fourteen, some explanation of or potential clue to an identity that marked him out from the world around him, from his neighbours, his classmates, his teachers, from the radio announcers, characters in films, the people my father used to see from the window of the bus walking back and forth and who never gave the matter a second's thought.

15.

My father began to take an interest in all this because of the death of my grandfather, which is perfectly understandable in the circumstances, because religion isn't something you think about when you're fourteen, even if that religion has the historical and cultural weight of Judaism, and even if my father had known that my grandfather's refusal to deal with the subject was not a mere whim, a personal choice made by a grown man, but the symptom of something that was doubtless apparent in the way he lived his life and the way he treated his wife and son and everyone.

16.

Wife — person who takes charge of all the domestic tasks, ensuring that the most rigorous standards of hygiene are employed in the house and that during the day her husband remains undisturbed whenever he wishes to be alone.

17.

I don't know when my grandfather began writing the notebooks, but it's likely that it was decades after the events he describes, at a time when it became his main aim in life to remain shut up in his study drafting these encyclopedic entries. Because the text doesn't change greatly as it progresses, as if it had been written in one go, and the pattern is set pretty much right from the start, with my grandfather talking about my grandmother and the sewing machine business that was so successful he was able to open a small shop in Porto Alegre shortly after my father was born.

18.

My father started working when he was fourteen, immediately after the death of my grandfather. Initially, my grandmother took over the running of the business, and I don't know if she helped him get his bearings then or not, because at fourteen there isn't much a boy can do in a shop apart from stocktaking or helping at the till or receiving orders or pretending that he's older than he is so as to be able to write out receipts, but I think the hustle and bustle and the customers' chatter and the visits to a tea shop two blocks away to eat cheesecake helped him get through those first few years and thus escape the grim prospect of having to come home from school and spend the evenings among furniture and objects that served only to remind him of my grandfather.

19.

In time, all this ceased to be pure therapy. My father came to enjoy the day-to-day life in the shop, and when he was eighteen or nineteen my grandmother left him in sole charge, and a few years later he opened another branch, then a second, then a third, and in each one he changed the merchandise. From sewing machines he moved on to fabrics, then to clothes, then to furniture and car parts, which meant that, by the time I was born, I was the heir to what had become a miniature empire.

20.

My father met my mother when he was nineteen, at a dance at the Jewish club. In those days, men still wore ties and women waited to be invited to take the floor, and it's always tempting to think about what might have been if something had gone wrong on that night, if something had interrupted the sequence of chance events that led to my birth. It's always tempting to imagine what my father felt when I was born, how he communicated those feelings to my mother and whether or not this determined the way

44

in which he related to me over the years. What child hasn't felt the same curiosity? And then I imagine the impact my grandfather's notebooks must have had on my father: it's possible there to retrace a similar path, with my grandfather describing my grandmother's pregnancy, what he referred to as *the pregnant wife*, the entry in which he writes that the wife should tell her husband about the pregnancy so that the husband can immediately take *the necessary decision*.

21.

It's tempting to say that my father's reaction to the notebooks influenced the way in which he dealt not only with Judaism but with everything else: his memory of my grandfather, his marriage to my mother, his way of relating to me at home, and since I never got to know another side to him, because he never showed me another side, it's clear that I, too, became caught up in that story.

22.

For me, everything begins when I was thirteen, at João's birthday party, when I let him fall. The head teacher summoned the parents of the boys who had been involved. The incident had occurred outside of school, but the staff-student coordinator nevertheless felt that it was within her jurisdiction. When my father asked me about it, he already knew that the other boys involved had told the coordinator it had been an accident, that we often played such pranks on each other and, up until then, no one had been hurt. My father was unconvinced by this explanation, he certainly didn't treat the matter as a mere childish prank, nor did he speak to me in a jokey, confiding way or tell me about something similar that had happened to him in the past, and he made me promise never to allow such a thing to happen again, but after that he said no more about it. In the months that followed, he showed no more interest than usual in school, my behaviour, my friends or João.

23.

At the time, he and João rarely met. In the afternoons, I would be left alone apart from the maid. João would arrive after lunch, it was exam month, and he was behind with his studies because of all the time he had spent recuperating. I helped him with Portuguese,

46

maths and science, and although this required work and effort on my part, I continued to copy out my notes for him, to talk about the books we had to read at home, to repeat what we had been taught in class, because otherwise it would be impossible for him to do the exercises.

24.

At around four or five, the maid would bring us our afternoon snack. I usually had a toasted banana sandwich and a milkshake, and we would stop for a rest. Unlike my other classmates, João didn't play video games. He had never used a videocassette player. He had never been in a house like mine, where, as soon as summer began, we could turn on the air conditioning, my room like an island where day by day, subject by subject, we worked our way through the study schedule, until the light changed and the temperature cooled and we could finally free ourselves from our textbooks and end the afternoon by the swimming pool.

25.

João did not belong to the same club as me, and had never jumped from a diving board

like the one we had at my house, a wall that
we would scale, putting our feet in the gaps
between the bricks, and from which you had
to jump, clearing the lawn and the plants
and the stones and the tiles around the edge
of the swimming pool, a jump I found
relatively easy, but which it took João a while
to screw up the necessary courage to make:
the almost two-metre-high wall, the sun going
down on the other side, the wind and the
mosquitoes and the smell of cut grass after a
long hot day, and me saying come on, it's not
that tricky, and him crouched, concentrated,
eyes wide, calf muscles tensed, a leap into
space as if there were no gravity and a fall
into the void taking care not to breathe out.

26.

Some people open their eyes underwater,
others prefer not to, and I don't know that it
makes much difference when you're plunging
down to the bottom and you have to wait
patiently until the impetus slows and you stop
in the middle of all the bubbles and allow
buoyancy to carry you back to the surface.
You propel your body upwards using long
movements of the arms, and you're very
conscious of your legs and your stomach, and

when you emerge into the light you look at the edge of the pool, and the colours have never seemed so bright, you're intensely aware of the reflections on the water that shines and laps against the tiles and the slap of the waves and the taste of chlorine in your nose, and then the fear you'd been feeling all afternoon and all the previous afternoons ever since the day of the fall at the birthday party vanishes as if you had been born again.

27.

It would be hard to say why I became João's friend. These things don't happen because you feel sorry for someone, or because you've spent months tormented by the idea that you almost destroyed that person, although it might help to begin with, at least as an impulse when you first decide to approach him. If it wasn't for that initial awkwardness, I wouldn't have offered to help him with his studies. If it weren't for those afternoons at my house, we wouldn't have spent so much time together. And if we hadn't done that, which happened in parallel with the whole recovery process, with his physiotherapy sessions, the exercises he did to strengthen his muscles, the press-ups and sit-ups and weightlifting which he started doing almost obsessively, I wouldn't have come to see what had previously seemed idiotic in João's personality as a quality.

28.

At the time, I spoke very little to my father. He would arrive home from work at night, exhausted, and by then I would have had my supper and would usually already be in bed asleep. If I were to calculate the amount of time we spent together each week, it would only be a few hours, and since included in those hours were his speeches about the Jews who died in the 1972 Olympics, the Jews who died in PLO attacks, the Jews who would continue to die because of the neo-Nazis in Europe and the Soviet alliance with the Arabs and the ineffectual stance taken by the UN and the media's negative attitude towards Israel, it's possible that more than half the conversations he had with me turned on that one topic.

29.

As a child, I used to dream about those stories, the swastikas and the Cossack torches outside the window, as if someone in the street were about to put me in a pair of pyjamas with a star on them and shove me onto a train headed for the chimneys, but this changed over the years. I realised that the stories kept being repeated, my father told them all in the same way, with the same intonation, and even today I can quote examples that would often cause his voice to break, the young girl who was imprisoned, the two brothers who were separated, the doctor and the teacher and the postman and the pregnant woman who crossed the whole of Poland only to be caught in an ambush in the forest. Something happens when you see your father repeating the same thing once, twice, five hundred times, and suddenly you can no longer sympathise or feel affected by something which, gradually, when you get to be thirteen, in Porto Alegre, living in a house with a swimming pool and having shown yourself capable of allowing a classmate to fall to the floor on his back at his birthday party — gradually, you realise that those stories bear very little relation to your own life.

30.

After I became friends with João, I started looking at my other friends, unable to understand why they had done that, and how they had managed to co-opt me as well, and I began to feel ashamed that I had ever shouted *son-of-a-bitch goy*, and this became mixed up with my growing feelings of discomfort around my father, a rejection of the performance he gave whenever he spoke of anti-Semitism, because I had nothing in common with the people he talked about apart from having been born Jewish, and I knew nothing about those people apart from the fact that they were Jews, and even though so many had died in the concentration camps it made no sense to be reminded of this every day.

31.

It made no sense that I had nearly left a classmate crippled because of that or because I had in some way been influenced by it — my father's speeches like a prayer before each meal, solidarity with the world's Jews and a promise that their suffering would never be repeated, when what I had been witnessing for months was the exact opposite: João alone against the mob, ignoring the humiliations, never giving the slightest indication of defeat when he was buried in the sand, and because of that memory and my awareness that he was not the coward, but rather the ten or fifteen of us boys surrounding him, because of that sense of shame that would cling to me for ever unless I did something about it, I decided to change schools at the end of the year.

A FEW THINGS I KNOW ABOUT MYSELF

1.

There are various ways of interpreting my grandfather's notebooks. One is to assume that he could not possibly have spent years devoting himself to the task, compiling a kind of treatise on how the world should be, with his interminable entries on the ideal city, the ideal marriage, the ideal wife, the wife's pregnancy *accompanied with diligence and love* by the husband, and never once mention the most important event of his life.

2.

I read just a small part of the notebooks, and I was the only person to do so apart from my father. He had them translated after my grandfather died and never told my grandmother. I can even understand his reasons and even understand that this embarrassed him in a way, but right from the start, the effect they had on me was quite different.

3.

My father was a fairly keen reader. Yet despite that, I can only remember him mentioning perhaps ten books during my adolescence. Maybe no more than five. And the reason I can only remember the title of one of those five, *If This Is a Man*, which he acquired in a foreign edition, is because he was constantly reading out the descriptions of how a concentration camp worked, the nights Primo Levi had to share his bed with a watchmaker, the stories about high and low numbers, jobs, uniforms, soup.

4.

My father quoted from *If This is a Man* during the first serious argument we had. It was in the second term of the year in which I had my bar mitzvah, when I told him I wanted to leave the school. By that time, things had already changed, I had severed all ties with my former friends. I didn't even talk to them and had already become accustomed to being ignored by them too: from one day to the next, people start turning their back on you, they stop phoning or asking you so much as to lend them a pencil and, in the space of a week, you no longer feel able to talk about this with anyone, a state of affairs that can easily last for what remains of your school life, because there's nothing more difficult when you're thirteen than changing your label.

5.

At thirteen I was the student who had been summoned by the coordinator to talk about João's fall. Before summoning the parents of the other boys involved, she had a talk with each of us, one by one, and I was the last. Her office was decorated with drawings that the younger children had done to celebrate the school's anniversary. My classmates waffled on to her, praising everything they saw in the room, what lovely drawings, it's amazing how creative children are nowadays, is that a cross or a plane? My classmates praised her clothes, her hair, her children's smiles in the framed photos, and nine out of ten times they managed to get away without having to sign the disciplinary card.

6.

Three signatures meant a suspension, but in some cases the punishment was applied immediately: no classes for two days, which wasn't so bad out of exam time, but obviously that wasn't the only thing that changed the way I was viewed at school. It wasn't just that the others who let João fall were punished. It was what happened at my meeting with the coordinator: I went into her room determined to say nothing, to keep repeating that it had been an accident, but she received me with a smile and offered me a cup of coffee and a piece of cake and started asking questions about João's party, and I began to remember the party all over again, and she kept talking and I felt no desire to praise the drawings and the photos, and I was troubled by her gentle tone of voice, asking me if I thought that had been a safe, sensible game to play, if it had occurred to me that I might hurt my classmate, if I knew that his family had difficulties paying the school fees, and at a certain point her questions and the memory of João's father at the party and the thought of him in the park selling candyfloss so that he could throw a birthday party where João would be humiliated by his classmates in front of his family became mingled with a feeling of faintness, and I began to think I was about to be ill, that I needed to lie down, needed air because the windows were all closed, and still she waited for an answer until she saw the blood drain from my face and then, almost at the same time as I was vomiting up the coffee and the cake and everything else I'd eaten during the previous two days, I told her that the story about the fall being an accident was a lie.

7.

My father asked what was wrong with school, and I felt unable to explain. I didn't want to tell him that after being sick and then recovering in the coordinator's office, I had told her all the details, about João being buried in the sand, about the plan to let him fall after we had given him the bumps, about everyone else who had been part of the plan and how we'd carried that plan out at the party. I didn't want to tell him that the news was all round the school within half an hour, and that the whole of the seventh grade knew I had told on my classmates, and that the coordinator had suspended everyone except me, and that I had got away with just a warning.

8.

In other schools there was an admissions period that began in November, with written exams, an interview, a visit and a chat with the student's parents. In Porto Alegre there were schools run by priests, by nuns, German schools, English schools, girls' schools, crammer schools, and João had done really well in the tests for one particular school that had an excellent record when it came to getting its students through the university entrance exam, and so it was easy for his father to secure him a scholarship with an equally favourable discount.

9.

I never had the chance to go to a school like yours, my father said. I only ever studied in schools where there were no other Jews. I was the only Jew out of five hundred students, he said, and you don't know what it's like to spend the whole day studying, knowing that at any moment someone is sure to remember that. One day, someone notices you for the first time and what he sees is that you're a Jew. Even if you make friends with everyone, that's what they'll always say. Even if you're top of the class in every subject, that's what they'll always throw in your face.

10.

My father used to say that Jews should always choose professions that can be practised in any circumstances, because from one moment to the next you could be forced to leave the country where you've always lived and you can't rely on a language that isn't spoken anywhere else, or on a knowledge of laws that don't apply anywhere else, that's why it's good to be a doctor or a dentist or an engineer or a tradesman, because that will guarantee you an income regardless of what the neighbours may say about you, and they'll say what people will always say about Jews, that you steal other people's jobs, that you lend money at interest, that you exploit, plot, threaten, oppress.

11.

I studied law at university, then went into journalism, and then became a writer, by which time my father had stopped staring at me, eyes bulging, as he tried to convince me that we were still in the Germany of 1937. When I was thirteen it was different, and because he wouldn't accept my decision to join João at the new school, because he refused to discuss the matter whenever I brought it up, because our arguments became so fierce that I was permanently grounded, with me telling him that I wouldn't study at all next term, that I would run away from home if he didn't change his mind and that he had a deadline by which to make a decision, the date on which enrolment at João's new school closed, for all those reasons I began to hate everything to do with Nazism and my grandfather.

12.

My father had my grandfather's notebooks translated because he needed a record of those memories, and because he was the only one who would be interested, a son reading the description of his own birth in his own father's words, my grandfather saying that *the birth of a child crowns a husband's decision to seal his union with his wife*, and that there is no happier event in a man's life than *the day he accompanies his wife to the hospital to give birth to a child.*

13.

My grandmother's pregnancy was high risk. She suffered from hypertension and had a problem with her cervix. It was fairly common at the time for there to be complications, deaths from eclampsia or a hospital infection picked up immediately after giving birth were far more frequent, and little was known about the effects of diabetes and heart problems and smoking and viruses on the health of the pregnant woman. The way people reacted to such risks was also quite different: it wasn't uncommon for a pregnancy to be terminated for fear the mother's life might be in danger, and my grandfather's descriptions of the time are all imbued with that subtext, what to do with my grandmother when the doctor recommended that she should spend the final months of her pregnancy at home, in bed if possible, without getting up and preferably without moving.

14.

What decision to take about a pregnancy that could have killed my grandmother? What did my grandfather say to her when he found out about this risk? How did my grandfather deal with the matter, what words did he use to express his wish to have a child at that moment, what did a child mean to him, would he be capable of devoting himself to a child, and because of that child forget about the past and all the dreadful things he had seen and suffered because of it?

15.

The same notebooks that describe a public baths in the centre of the Porto Alegre of 1945 as *a place where the most rigorous hygiene regime flourishes*, a butcher's shop attached to a poultry slaughterhouse in the Porto Alegre of 1945 as *a business where the animals are treated according to the most rigorous of hygiene regimes*, a kennels in the Porto Alegre of 1945 as a place where *the animals are treated according to the most rigorous and humane of hygiene regimes*, those same notebooks say that the decision to go ahead with my grand-mother's pregnancy was taken *without hesitation* and speak of *the expectation of a new life that had long been planned* by the husband and of *his profound desire for continuity and a loving, giving relationship.*

16.

Hospital — *a place where doctors patiently explain to the pregnant woman the very low* degree of risk involved in any pregnancy and the equally low risk involved in having a Caesarean and the non-existent risk of infection after the birth given the hospital's rigorous hygiene procedures which extend to the bathrooms with hot running water and to the toilets which are cleaned every hour, and to the care assistants who apply these rigorous hygiene procedures throughout the day, using disinfectants, sterilising agents and quarantine. There is nothing at the hospital that need trouble the husband of the pregnant woman, whose child will put the seal on the continuity of their loving, giving relationship should he choose to walk down the corridor alone or go home in order to be alone.

17.

My grandfather continues to discourse upon the ideal baby, how to care for the ideal baby, the father's relationship with the ideal baby, a small autonomous creature who never cries at night and never contracts diseases such as hepatitis or the common cold, and the truly alarming thing is that he filled sixteen notebooks, measuring twenty-eight centimetres by nineteen, each with nearly one hundred pages, each page having thirty-one lines, filled with a prose that leaves no doubt as to how my grandfather dealt with his memories.

18.

My father was born at five o'clock on a Monday afternoon, but I don't know if the day was sunny or gloomy, cold or hot, dry or humid, because my grandfather doesn't bother to mention it. My grandfather filled sixteen notebooks without once saying what he felt about my father, not one honest, open remark, not one word of the kind one usually finds in the memoirs of concentration camp survivors, about how life goes on after you leave a place like Auschwitz, the renewal of hope when they have a child after leaving Auschwitz, the rediscovery of joy on seeing that child growing up like a riposte to everything they saw in Auschwitz, and just the horror of knowing that someone survived Auschwitz only to waste all their free time on that sterile enterprise, on the pointless, inexplicable exercise of imagining every real phenomenon as something to be transformed into its exact opposite, to the point that all defects, all features disappear, along with the characteristics that allow those things and places and people to be appreciated for what they really are, that horror must somehow be related to Auschwitz and to the way in which my grandfather always behaved towards my father.

19.

I've never asked my father what memories he has of his childhood, if my grandfather sang the lullabies that Jewish parents used to sing to their children before Auschwitz was built, if my grandfather embraced him as Jewish parents used to embrace their children before Auschwitz was opened, if my grandfather defended him as Jewish parents throughout history used to defend their children before Auschwitz was functioning at full capacity, because that is what a father does for a child, he protects and teaches and showers him with affection and with physical and material comforts, and the way in which my father dealt with the subject of Judaism and the concentration camps must, in some way, be connected to those memories — how he related what he saw and knew and felt about my grandfather with what he read and knew and felt about Auschwitz.

20.

It's difficult to say what my first memory of my father is. It's possible that you associate a smell or a taste or a sensation of warmth with the evocation of something you would have no way of holding in your memory, as if you were looking at yourself from the outside, in a cradle beside your father's bed, and you talk about it because it's a relatively common scene, and innumerable emotional and cultural references mean that the initial relationship between father and baby should, in some way, be linked to that scene, the cradle and the blankets and the smile of someone whom you sense or know is as close to you as anyone can be.

21.

I'm incapable of remembering what my father smelled like when I was a child. People's smell changes with age, just as their skin and their voice change too, and when you speak of your childhood it may be that you associate the image of your father then with the image you have of your father now. And so when I remember him bringing me a tricycle as a present, or showing me how a sewing machine works, or asking me to read out a few words from the newspaper, or talking to me about the things one talks about with a child of three, four, seven, thirteen, when I remember all those things the image I have of him is the image I have of him today, his hair and face, my father much thinner and wearier and more bent than he is in old photos that I've only ever seen at most five times in my life.

22.

When I remember my father forbidding me to change schools, the voice I hear is his voice today, and I wonder if something similar is happening with him: if the memory he has of me at thirteen gets confused with the image he has of me now, after everything he has learned about me in the last almost three decades, an accumulation of facts that erase all the stumbling blocks along the road to here, and if what I experienced as a decisive chapter in my life, the argument we had over my wanting to change schools, might for him be merely a banal fact, one of the many things that happened at home and at work and in the life he had with my mother and with the other people who were around during his son's adolescence.

23.

During the quarrel we had over the new school, I told my father that I didn't give a toss about his arguments, that using Judaism as an argument for not changing schools was ridiculous. I said I didn't give a toss about Judaism, still less about what had happened to my grandfather. It isn't the same thing as saying out loud that you hate someone and wish them dead, but anyone who has a relative who spent time in Auschwitz can confirm the rule that, from childhood on, you know that you can speak lightly about anything but that, and so my father's reaction to my remark was predictable enough, repeat what you just said, go on if you're brave enough, and I looked him straight in the eye and said, very slowly this time, that he could stick Auschwitz and Nazism and my grandfather up his arse.

24.

My father had never laid a hand on me before, and it may be that I was one of those children who had been spoiled by not having been brought up with strict enough boundaries, a rich little thirteen-year-old who wasn't used to being given a slap and to accepting that this was simply the way things are, and even if the slap hadn't really hurt and I'd been tall enough or strong enough to inflict some damage on my father in any physical confrontation, the normal response would have been for me to recoil before that show of authority. But that isn't what happened: he hurled himself upon me and I tried to extricate myself, then he got a firm hold on me and hit me several times, on the back, on the neck, until his anger passed and he slowly loosened his grip and lay me down on the ground, my ears burning, a breathing space before I could get to my feet, my whole body trembling, and finally pull myself together.

25.

Even now I still wonder what would have happened if there had been no fight, if my father hadn't changed as if overnight and stopped talking to me about my grandfather, as though the fight had created a tacit understanding, with him sensing that it wasn't Nazism and Auschwitz that were at stake, because I knew very little about Nazism and Auschwitz, but whatever it was that I felt to be at the root of what had happened to João.

26.

If I were to talk now to any of the classmates who were involved in João's fall, it's likely that none of them would remember the details of the party or the reasons that led us to hatch that plan, and that none of them would make the link between carrying it out and the fact that João was not a Jew, because social conventions and the rules of etiquette and the self-image that each would have constructed of himself over the ensuing years would have created defence mechanisms that prevented their memory from recording something like that.

27.

It's possible that the same applies to everyone who had anything to do with the school, classmates, parents of classmates, the staff-student coordinator, the teachers, they might even say that my version of the story was a distortion, a false memory influenced by my subsequent feelings, the trauma of spending a year dreaming over and over about João's fall, because it's ridiculous even to think that such a thing could happen in the 1980s in a Jewish school in Porto Alegre, a place attended by the sons of tradesmen and factory-owners and members of the liberal professions who had always lived alongside non-Jews, and there's no record of any discrimination against Jews in the Porto Alegre of the time, no club that excluded Jews, no politician who spoke ill of Jews, no one who in the presence of family or friends or customers would dare say anything against the Jews, so it simply doesn't make sense to think that the opposite could also happen, and if, say, such a thing were said at some point as a joke at school, that was no reason for someone to get so upset that it would cause him to change the way he lived the rest of his life.

28.

In the case of my father, I don't know if he changed because of the fight itself and because he went to bed that night troubled by the fact of having attacked his thirteen-year-old son for the first time ever, a shock to the self-image he had created up until then, to his certain belief that he would never be capable of hurting his son, or because pushing me and grabbing me around the neck and punching me could not only have caused injury, it was also capable of provoking in me an entirely unforeseeable reaction — and so I don't know whether he went to bed troubled by the fact of having attacked me or by that reaction.

29.

Until João's fall, I had never done anything like that either or even felt capable of it. My father was in the doorway staring at me perplexed, once I'd got to my feet after he stopped hitting me and I was aware of the pain and the possible bruises and an anger I had never felt before, and even today I can still remember the look of alarm on his face when I picked up the first thing to hand, one of those heavy Sellotape dispensers with sharp enough edges to dent someone's head or put out their eye, and at that moment it was as if I were taking my revenge for everything that had happened that year, my classmates, the staff-student coordinator, my father who seemed so vulnerable, and if he hadn't managed to step out of the way or if I hadn't miscalculated when I threw the Sellotape dispenser or a combination of both those things, that could have been the second tragedy of the year.

30.

The day after the fight, my father told me all the details of my grandfather's story. I had spent the day in my room, and he knocked on the door and said we had to talk. He sat down on a stool by my bed and, after apologising, he then politely told me off for what I'd said and done, and asked that it never happen again because he was too old for that kind of thing and, besides, there was my mother to consider, and I could almost swear that in his voice there was not just guilt or sadness or disappointment, but an embarrassed kind of fear, as if he had found something out about me, a secret that had lain hidden for years, the threat inside his own house.

31.

My father told me about my grandfather's final days, and that was enough for me to understand that I should never again treat the matter lightly. I realised that this was something I should respect as much as my father respected my right to study at a new school and, after that tacit agreement, my relationship with him became quite different: on that day my anger vanished, and in the weeks that followed it was as if everything went back to how it used to be before João's fall, family suppers, weekends, the conversations in which I said little and simply listened to what my father had to say, although he was no longer trying to convince me of anything or condemning me for wanting to take the entrance exams for a school where there were no Jews, and for being admitted into a school where there were no Jews, and getting enrolled and waiting for the start of term at a school where I thought no one would ever even mention Jews, a story that could have remained frozen there, forgotten, if it hadn't resurfaced decades later, when I was an adult and had left home, changed cities and become another person: João, my grandfather, Auschwitz and the notebooks, I only started thinking about all this again when I found out that my father was ill.

NOTES (1)

My father gave me a tricycle when I was three, and the tricycle made the rattling sound you get when you tie the lid from a margarine carton to the rim of a bicycle wheel. The tricycle doubled as a truck and had a trailer too, into which I would put whatever I happened to find around the house: cushions, plates, towels, candles, a bottle of shampoo, and I would tell my father that I was delivering goods to various cities, and he would say, that's more or less what your grandfather did when he first arrived in Brazil.

In every photo of my grandfather he's wearing a suit and there's no sign of the number tattooed on him at Auschwitz. My grandmother's photographs were in frames on a shelf beside the table. All the furniture in my grandmother's apartment was made of dark wood: chairs, a coffee table, a dressing table. Her bed was narrow and very soft, and it resembled my grandmother's hair, almond brown and cotton white with a touch of purple, and after lunch on a winter's day I used to enjoy lying there, reading comics.

I learned to read before I went to school, and my father would practise with me, showing me words in the newspaper and saying, what letter is that, and they were printed letters, quite different from the ones I would learn in the primer that schools used at the time, the *a* has its tummy on this side, without a back it's a *c*, and with its tummy on the other side it's a *b*, the snake is an *s*, and the noise the snake makes before it attacks is *sssss* but when it's sleeping *zzzzzz*, and the first word I read was *house*, and fixed to the edge of the writing desk where my father would sit to read the newspaper was a pencil sharpener with a handle, I remember the pencil box, the sound of the blade cutting into the wood, the effort involved, the blister on my finger.

My father would explain to me how sewing machines worked, about the thread, the engine, the different sorts of needle for backstitch, buttons, synthetics, embroidery, leather, and the pieces of cloth I would hold in my hand, eyes closed, while my father asked me, what is it, and I would have to say it's linen, silk, synthetic, and when I was about ten years old I went to the main shop in the centre of town, and my father summoned one of the shop assistants and made me repeat the experiment in front of him, and then the assistant took me out for an ice cream while my father stayed in the office, talking on the phone and endlessly tapping away on a calculator.

My father would come and pick me up from the rabbi's house and he always asked, what did you learn today, and I would say, nothing, I just learned by heart a load of words I don't even know the meaning of, and he would say, the rabbi should explain what those passages from the Torah mean. Every Saturday when someone is bar-mitzvahed, a different text is read out, and it's only at the actual ceremony that you touch the parchment itself, which is very white with the Hebrew characters printed or hand-written on it, with polished batons attached to the scrolls and a velvet cover to protect it from the light, and there you are in suit and shoes and a white tallit with a sky-blue pattern and a suede kippah with a gold sequin on top.

My school was on three floors and had a high wall around it and on the pavement outside there were flower planters on which the paint was almost concealed under a layer of dust, and which were, in fact, disguised steel blocks that reached two and a half metres down to protect the building against bomb attacks.

João always wore a crumpled plain T-shirt.

I never saw him wearing one with a design on it. That was the present my mother bought for him, the fashion at the time was for surfing images, Rio de Janeiro landmarks, a seagull, a flash of lightning, a fishing pier.

The floor of the reception room where João's birthday was held was tiled. He fell with a thud, which I heard because I was standing so close and because everyone had just finished shouting out *thirteen*, just a moment after the final syllable, which is usually more drawn out, either from enthusiasm or habit or perhaps anger.

When we left the party, we took a taxi. The taxis in Porto Alegre in the 1980s were rather drab, and the brake pedal made a noise like an old spring being released, which I suspect the drivers rather liked because they made a point of bringing up the pedal really quickly. The drivers sat on sheepskin seat covers in the cold weather and hung crab claws or images of saints on the rear-view mirror.

While João was recovering I went to school and spent the morning alone, and during break I stayed in the classroom and ate a sandwich, because I'd started bringing my lunch from home, and sometimes the flask containing my cold drink would leak because I hadn't closed the lid properly, and the butter and cheese and lettuce would end up sodden and sweet.

I can't remember if it was hot or cold on the day I apologised to João. The first time he dived into our swimming pool the weather was as stifling as if it were January. Whenever João came to my house, he would show me the exercises he was doing, three hundred push-ups with his arms spread wide, as well as sit-ups and stretches, the equipment in the fitness room at the school gym was rather antiquated, with free weights and no lumbar supports.

On the few occasions I went to the coordinator's office, the photographs were always the same, her son wearing a pirate hat, her daughter in a ballet outfit, and the drawings on the wall didn't change either: paper kites, mountains, houses with one window above the front door, a smiling sun with eyes and hair.

When you're known as a snitch, people eye you scornfully, but that isn't always evident in the look on their face or some movement of their mouth or eyebrows, because very few show their feelings so overtly, and still fewer say anything beyond what those involved had already said, the other four who came to speak to me one by one and called me a son-of-a-bitch.

The way my father immobilised me on the

day of the fight: his right arm wrapped around my neck, while he used his left to hit me.

The dispenser I threw at him had a roll of Sellotape in it at the time. The acrylic base was about twenty centimetres long, weighed maybe two kilos, and the cutting edge had small metal teeth.

When my father came to speak to me on the day after the fight, he knocked three times on my bedroom door. My father was never ill when I was a child. He was never ill when I was fifteen, eighteen or twenty-five, and I don't remember him being ill when he was fifty, fifty-five, sixty.

When I found out about my father's illness, it was three o'clock in the afternoon and I went into a bar and ordered a beer. I drank the beer and ordered a whisky. The whisky immediately warmed me up, ethanol on a sunny day at a bar with a few nibbles and a sweet-vending machine.

I thought about my father while I drank the whisky. And I thought I really should stop drinking. And I ordered another whisky, and then another and another, and the hours passed and then a moment came when I remembered what had happened, and I couldn't possibly go home in that state because I didn't want to explain and discuss the details of my father's medical tests with anyone.

The lights at night are blurred and you walk along talking to yourself. It's almost a joy to do that, knowing that no one is listening. One block before you reach a park. The damp, muggy air and the bus fumes. Fresh mud after the last rain shower. The scratched surface of a bench, no animals around, the results of my father's tests in an envelope, just me and the silence, me lying down and the sense of imminent physical torpor, just relax and close your eyes and imagine some dark, isolated place and a warm, slow, constant rocking taking you nowhere.

A FEW MORE THINGS I KNOW ABOUT MY GRANDFATHER

1.

I found out that my father had Alzheimer's two years ago. One day, when he was driving just a few blocks away from our house, he suddenly felt lost and couldn't think how to get home. It was a brief, isolated episode, but when he kept forgetting small things, where his keys were, a suit he'd sent to the dry cleaner's, often enough for my mother to notice, she helped me persuade him to seek help. I had never before taken my father to the doctor, and, as far as I knew, he went for regular check-ups for blood, heart and prostate.

2.

Alzheimer's is a disease whose mechanisms are not yet fully known, although two proteins have been linked to its appearance, tau and beta-amyloid, which are responsible for cell structure and for transporting fat to the nuclei of cells. In Alzheimer's patients these proteins deposit fat in and around the neurones, thus suffocating them. Age is one of the risk factors, but a healthy lifestyle associated with specific intellectual activities can help postpone its initial evolution.

3.

I like talking and reading about medicine, although neurology has never been an area of particular interest to me. In recent years, I've had labyrinthitis, gastritis, conjunctivitis and sinusitis. I've also had a broken finger, sciatica, a sprained ankle, and a late case of chickenpox. As well as bouts of arrhythmia and what the doctors call presyncope, a minor heart problem for which there is little point taking any medication and whose symptoms are negligible, and for at least a year now I've been experiencing a recurrent cough and persistent tiredness, which could be attributed to stress, a sedentary job or alcohol abuse.

4.

I started drinking when I was fourteen, after João and I changed schools. I'd had the occasional beer with my father and the occasional glass of wine at some grown-up suppers at home, but the first time I got seriously drunk was at a party just after term started. I didn't go straight to the party, but to the house of a classmate whose parents were out and, when we left there, some of the boys were singing and talking loudly, and I climbed into the taxi clutching a plastic bottle cut in half. Someone had mixed *cachaça* and Coca-Cola, and you had to hold your breath every time you took a swig of it, and when I got out of the taxi, my legs felt hollow and by then everyone was laughing and it was easy enough to spend the rest of the night leaning against a wall next to a speaker. I mixed *cachaça* with vodka and with some cheap wine that stained your teeth purple, and by eleven o'clock I'd crawled out into the garden and found a dark corner where I sat, feeling rather weak, and where no one would find me once I'd slid helplessly to the ground, because I still didn't really know any of my classmates.

5.

It was a while before my classmates asked if I was Jewish, because identifying surnames is something that only older people and Jews in general do, and my name doesn't end in *man* or *berg* or any of those other telltale suffixes that would have given a clue to anyone who didn't know where I'd studied before. In the lessons at the new school, the Holocaust was only mentioned in passing as an episode in the Second World War, and Hitler was analysed through the historical lens of the Weimar Republic, the economic crisis of the 1930s, and the soaring inflation that obliged people to use wheelbarrows to carry their money back from the market, a story that aroused so much interest that you reached the final year of school knowing more about how quick shoppers had to be if they wanted to reach the cashier before the price of bread or milk went up again than about how prisoners were transported to the concentration camps. Not one of the teachers gave more than a cursory nod to Auschwitz. Not one of them said a word about *If This Is a Man*. Not one of them made the obvious calculation that a fourteen-year-old like me must have had a father or a grandfather or a great-grandfather or a cousin or a friend of a friend of a friend who had escaped the gas chambers.

6.

I don't know if my grandfather ever read *If This is a Man* or if the fact of having actually lived through what Primo Levi wrote about would have made him read the book differently, whether what was a revelation to the ordinary reader, a detailed description of the whole Auschwitz experience, would have been merely a process of recognition for my grandfather, a matter of checking to see whether or not the book corresponded to reality or to the reality of his memory, and I don't know to what extent that somewhat distanced reading would reduce the book's impact.

7.

I don't know how my grandfather used to react when he heard a joke about Jews, assuming anyone ever told such jokes to him, or if he, as the distracted guest at some cocktail party or supper or business meeting, was ever in a room where someone was telling them and where he might have heard a high-pitched giggle in response to the word *Jew* — or what his reaction would have been to knowing that this is what happened to me when I was fourteen, that this was the

nickname that began to be used as soon as
João mentioned our previous school with
the little synagogue in the grounds and the
seventh-grade students studying for their bar
mitzvah, and that the nickname meant
something different for me, that instead of
feeling angry at an insult that ought to be
confronted or indignant at the implied
stereotype — the old men all in black and
with vampire teeth and speaking in a foreign
accent who used to appear in films and TV
soaps — I preferred not to say or do
anything, at least initially.

8.

It's not difficult to explain that attitude: you
just have to imagine changing schools, the
passing of a few months during which
someone does sit-ups and weightlifting and
his voice breaks and he grows ten centimetres
before he meets his new classmates, and all it
takes in the first week is for one of those
classmates to try and provoke João and for
João to respond and for the classmate to raise
his voice and for João to raise his voice too,
and it's as if we were back in the playground
at the old school during the same break-time
and with the same bullying classmate, except

that João is taller and stronger now and knows he has little to lose apart from getting a warning or a trip to the first-aid room to have a Band-aid applied to his head, and there I am watching João doing exactly what he should have done the year before, you only have to react once, you just have to close your eyes and launch yourself at the person provoking you and grab him by the throat or sink your teeth into him and tear a piece out of him if necessary, just once, and no one will ever again call you weak or scared or a goy or a Jewish son-of-a-bitch.

9.

Just once, and in the weeks that follow everything changes, the first party, João and me in the middle of the small group who went to the classmate's house whose parents were away, sixty guests at the party and our small group arriving slightly late, João ten centimetres taller now and with no trace of what happened to him in the previous year, the music, the dance floor, the girls, me and the ice chest and the plastic cup and the speaker, me drinking one cup after another while João was dancing as if he'd never eaten sand, going over to one of the girls, hands on hips, as if he'd never been buried in the sand, the way he turns his head, the words he whispers in her ear, João taking the girl by the hand as if he'd never fallen flat on his back at his own birthday party in front of his father and sixty other people who would never believe what I was seeing now, while I had already gone out into the garden, already found a dark corner, was already lying beneath a tree while the world was spinning and I could feel only the damp grass and my throat and my stomach as I watched João approach with the girl and lean her against the tree before leaning against her.

10.

What can change in a matter of months? A ten-centimetre growth spurt. A deeper voice. An older face. When you're fourteen, you can easily get strong doing push-ups and weight-lifting, and that in itself gives you extra confidence if anyone should make a snide comment about you, and just the way you turn your head will determine whether what the person said will be passed off as a joke or never again repeated, and just the way you walk and lean casually on the speaker and behave with girls at a party will determine how the rest of your year will go, you who were in the majority at the school where you both studied before, you who had more friends at the school where you both studied before, who did what you liked throughout your years at the school where you both studied before, *Jew*, but if all that ends, you become the one dependent on your friend, the one who gets invited to a classmate's house because of him, the one they put up with, and you have to accept the fact that they only talk to you because he does.

11.

I doubt that João ever read *If This is a Man*, and it's possible that he would never have considered what an Auschwitz survivor would say about being diagnosed with Alzheimer's, knowing that in a few years he would forget everything: childhood, school, the first time a neighbour was arrested, the first time a neighbour was sent to a concentration camp, the first time you heard the name Auschwitz and realised that it would stay with you for a very long time, your fellow prisoners in Auschwitz, the guards at Auschwitz, the people who died in Auschwitz, the meaning of that word disappearing into a limbo outside the eternal present that will gradually become your sole reality.

12.

I was the one who told my father he had Alzheimer's. I talked to him about the initial stages of the illness, about the long period of time that would pass before the symptoms got worse, and that was all I could do because in two clicks of a mouse my father had access to any website describing the condition in detail: photos of patients, always the same blank gaze and the sense that something is missing from the photo, the relatives out of sight, behind the camera in the hospital room or kilometres away if possible, in another city so as not to run the risk of having to make a Sunday visit and find their father reduced to a pair of blue pyjamas, a figure with short hair, a sheet and the gaze of someone who no longer knows what a camera or a photograph is, like a baby in front of a mirror with no notion yet that the reflection contains the image we have and will have of ourselves until everything begins to change.

13.

The image I had of myself on the day I told my father he had Alzheimer's was this: a man nearing forty, who had been reasonably successful in his career, who had published books that had enjoyed a reasonably warm critical reception, and who managed to get on reasonably well with the people to whom he was close, writers, publishers, translators, agents, journalists or friends he had lunch with twice a year but whose wife's or children's names he didn't know, friends whose habits and plans and conversations had long since ceased to interest him.

14.

At nearly forty, I was on my third marriage. The first lasted three years. I was twenty-one when we met and I made all the mistakes one would expect in that situation. It was a prolonged period of mutual incomprehension, and now I feel neither regret nor pain nor tenderness when I think of that time.

15.

The second marriage lasted even less time, two years out of a total of six years spent together, and which ended in more or less the same way, but afterwards I would often remember the apartment we lived in, the trips we made, the friends we had in common, the things she would tell me about her work and that I would tell her about mine, the dinner parties we gave, the Sunday mornings spent reading the paper, me snuggled up close to her beneath the sheets one night when the hail was beating so hard against the shutters we thought the building was going to collapse, her family, her clothes, the films and books she liked, her voice, her hair, the shape of her fingers, the little groan she gave when she stretched, and all the infinite number of details that were lost because we never spoke to each other again.

16.

None of the women I married knew anything about João. Once I grew up, I never talked about him or about my first weeks at the new school, the new classmates who drank and smoked hash and sniffed glue and benzine, and went out in the late afternoon setting fire to litter bins and stealing tokens from public phone boxes. You have to rip the whole apparatus off the wall, leaving only a stub of cable, and you stand close by the classmate who's doing this, then run off with him to a safe place where someone with a screwdriver and a hammer and a chisel breaks through the outer shell into the box containing a handful of tokens that will never be of any use, and although none of that should have struck me as new in relation to what I'd more or less experienced during the previous year, it did. The new school was a hostile environment in a different way, and that wasn't just because of the way my classmates looked at me and talked to me, but also the way in which João dealt or appeared to deal with it.

17.

João never talked to me in detail about the months that followed the fall. He forgave me so easily, became my friend so easily, accepted my decision to go with him to the new school, a thirteen-year-old saint who never expressed the least surprise at what I'd done and never told me what he really felt during that time: if he had dreams too, if he also relived the moment of the fall each night, if the thud on the floor had sounded the same to him as to me, and if seeing the scene from below had the same effect — if, in his dream, the people at the party were wearing tallits and kippahs, like an army formed up around the throne of David, with me standing above the throne holding an open Torah, and it's then that the door opens and João sees his father enter pushing a wheelchair, his father surrounded by nurses who all look at João and smile and put João in the wheelchair and the next scene is João in the classroom with his atrophied legs and his toes turned in and his arms grown strong from pushing the wheelchair back and forth.

18.

João never knew that I fought with my father because of all this. That I hurled a Sellotape dispenser at him because of all this. That for a moment there was a chance I could have hit my father on the head and injured his face, resulting in an operation on the cheekbone under general anaesthetic, leaving him with one eye that he would never be able to open again and all because my father — with his stories about the Holocaust and the Jewish renaissance and the obligation every Jew in the world had to defend himself using whatever means he had — was in some way responsible for what happened to João, making him the enemy who will always be there before you and who will always be in your thoughts because now he's in a wheelchair.

19.

I never told João that the quarrel with my father was the closest physical contact I'd had with him for thirteen years. On the day I found out he had Alzheimer's, I went to a bar and ordered a whisky and then another and then several more and ended up leaving the bar and sleeping on a park bench. When I woke it was broad daylight and I was filled with a feeling of immense weariness when I thought about how I was going to break the news to my father, and I remember that one of the things I thought was whether or not I would touch him when I gave him the news, whether I would take his hand or place my hand on his shoulder or give him a hug or attempt a smile indicating a minimum of optimism about the initial prognosis.

20.

I never told João what happened to me after I saw him fall. Surely he must have thought about it. Did he, for example, imagine that I became his friend out of pity? Or out of guilt? Or because I was alone and no one else would speak to me after my conversation with the coordinator? Or for any one of those reasons that would justify the resentment that would perhaps have remained hidden had it not been for the new circumstances, the new school, the new classmates, the numerous friends he'd never had before and who allowed him to do something he had perhaps always wanted to do, a month after the start of term, two months, then three, and there comes a moment when João realises that he doesn't need me any more, that I serve only as a reminder of the worst moment of his life, and he needs to move on from that memory and it's then that he can do something he's been planning for a long time, the one occasion on which he doesn't bother to lie when his new classmates ask him about the previous year.

21.

I'm not sure whether it happened in March or in April or at the latest in May, João telling them about the birthday party, the one occasion on which he let it slip in the middle of the jokes they had got used to making about me, at least they would sound like jokes now, after all the years that have passed and all the times someone has looked at me and talked about money and about a conspiracy by the rats that have infested our houses ever since the Middle Ages and spread discord and hatred among decent people. I wasn't there on the day, of course, and it wasn't perhaps João's deliberate intention, not directly anyway, but the fact is that it became public knowledge that I had allowed him to fall at his birthday party, my Jewish rat paws letting go of his head, my Jewish rat instinct fleeing in the ensuing confusion, my parasitic moneymaking cancerous Jewish rat nature betraying the rest of the gang in order to save myself and to continue sucking other people's blood and health.

22.

The next day everyone at school knew about it, but this time I was prepared, as if anaesthetised by what I'd experienced the previous year and which I would clearly go through again: the way people immediately changed the subject whenever I came into view, my name and the Star of David chalked on the wall in the corridor, and this time I myself would quickly rub it off so that no teacher would see it, so that the coordinator at the new school wouldn't call me into her office and express her profound regret at that display of religious and cultural intolerance, and so that faced by the coordinator's sympathy I wouldn't again run the risk of feeling sick and vomiting up the names of the classmates I believed had done it, or even giving João's name, because he must have known who was doing it, João who now only spoke to me in class or when we were alone together, where he wouldn't have to demonstrate in public that he had been or still was my friend or feel obliged to invite me to some party at the weekend, and gradually I would cease to know anything about João's life outside school, if he was still stealing tokens from public phone boxes, if he was still smoking hash and sniffing glue, if he had a girlfriend and was the first in the class to have one, and I started going straight from school to home and from home to school, cut off from João and all my other classmates and from any other possibility apart from studying and my bedroom and my life, which didn't change throughout the eternity of every day, every hour of eighth grade.

A FEW MORE THINGS I KNOW
ABOUT MY FATHER

1.

Of the six hundred and fifty Jews sent to Auschwitz along with Primo Levi, six hundred and thirty-eight died within the first year. Of the twelve who survived, Primo Levi was the only one to write a book, *If This Is a Man*. Unlike my grandfather, he was concerned with recording every detail of the camp routine, from his arrival in 1944 to his liberation by the Red Army when the war ended.

2.

Before *If This Is a Man*, no one knew about the card placed beside a tap just inside Auschwitz, warning inmates not to drink from it because the water was dirty. The rules also forbade sleeping in your jacket or without your underpants, or leaving the hut with your collar turned up or not taking a shower on the prescribed days.

3.

Fingernails needed to be trimmed regularly, but that could only be done with your teeth. With toenails, the friction of the shoes was enough. The shoes were distributed in a completely arbitrary fashion, and each prisoner had only a few seconds in which to choose, from a distance, a pair that appeared to be the right size, for there could be no changing them later, and according to Primo Levi, this was the first important decision to be made, because a shoe that is too tight or too loose causes blisters that burst and in turn cause infections that make the feet swell and stop you walking or running, and the rubbing of the swollen foot against the wood and cloth of the shoes causes more blisters and more infections that end up taking the prisoner to the hospital with a diagnosis of swollen feet, a complaint for which there is no cure in Auschwitz.

4.

Primo Levi says that in Auschwitz death begins with the shoes, and I wonder if he was referring only to his time in the camp or to the decades that passed after putting on the pair he managed to grab during those five decisive seconds. Primo Levi died when he was sixty-eight, in Turin, Italy, having written thirteen books, many of them about the Holocaust and many of which had been translated into various languages, and having resumed his career as a chemist, and married and had children and received prizes and become a literary celebrity in Europe and the world, and I wonder: was he thinking about that choice of shoe, too large or too small, or perhaps, with rare and enviable luck among the million and a half prisoners who passed through the camp, a shoe that was just the right size, was he thinking about that when he opened the door of his apartment, walked over to the stairs and fell down the stairwell, an occurrence that almost none of his biographers believes to have been accidental.

5.

Death begins in many ways, and I don't know if my grandfather ever managed to pinpoint the seed, the crucial moment when it ceased to matter that he had survived Auschwitz who knows how, and left there in who knows what state, and recovered in Poland or in Germany or who knows where, and managed to get himself on a boat heading for Brazil after overcoming who knows what difficulties, because from that moment on it was pretty clear that he would spend the rest of his life much as Primo Levi did. The only difference is that, instead of leading an apparently normal family life and decades later throwing himself down a stairwell, he led an apparently normal family life and decades later began writing those notebooks.

6.

Milk — a liquid food with a creamy texture, which as well as containing calcium and other substances essential to the organism has the advantage of not being highly susceptible to the development of bacteria. Milk is the perfect source of nourishment to be taken by a man when he is about to spend the morning alone.

7.

I saw a film once in which the son goes into his father's office and discovers that all the drawers are filled with loose cigarettes arranged in neat rows, this happens the day after his father has had a nervous breakdown in the shower and smashed the glass door, and I wonder if something similar occurred with my father when he read the first page or the first line of those sixteen notebooks.

8.

Sesefredo — guesthouse in the centre of Porto Alegre, a clean spacious establishment, quiet in the mornings and cosy and welcoming when night falls, located in a building which is per- fectly solid despite having survived a fire and which has a pleasant aspect to the sun, located in a street full of commercial establishments of unimpeachable reputation such as a kennels and a butcher's shop. Any guest of the Sesefredo who falls ill is sure to be well treated thanks to its owners' kindness which manifests itself in their sympathetic, cordial manners, in German, and with a rigorous attention to hygiene during the period in which, due to his need for healthful repose, he cannot be disturbed while alone in his room.

9.

Kennels — a place of long, brightly lit corri- dors run by professionals of the highest human and social calibre and where the animals are treated according to the most rigorous and humane of hygiene regimes. Anyone visiting the kennels will be provided with all the information he requires on the health of the animals as well as their legal position and the necessary adoption procedures and he can enjoy the small lawned courtyard and the wooden bench where a man who wants to sit there alone will be undisturbed by the noise of barking or other disagreeable sounds.

10.

Pregnancy — condition in which the wife spends entire months without a single illness and in no danger of diseases of the uterus or of high blood pressure. The wife learns she is pregnant and immediately tells her husband so that he can take the necessary decision: to have the child or not? A decision taken by him without hesitation because it crowns the expectation of a new life that has long been planned by him, his profound desire for continuity and a loving, giving relationship. His wife's pregnancy is observed with joy on his part and accompanied by him with diligence and love, confirming the good luck he has always enjoyed in life. During the wife's pregnancy, she is directed by the doctor and by her husband to apply the most rigorous hygiene procedures during the

pregnancy, making due use in the home
of alcohol and disinfectant, laundry soap,
brooms, mops and various kinds of cloth.
The wife's sole preoccupation during the preg-
nancy should be to ensure that her husband is
given the necessary peace and quiet when he
wishes to remain alone in his room or study.

11.

My father told me about the notebooks in
the conversation we had after the fight, when
I was thirteen. Up until then, he had kept
them a secret, ashamed to show me or anyone
else the proof that my grandfather had spent
his final years in the manner one would expect
of someone writing those entries — the period
when my grandfather would allow no one to
enter the study where he spent all day, the
endless days necessary to complete what he
must originally have intended to be far more
than those sixteen volumes, and I can imagine
my grandfather planning to create an entire
encyclopedia, *as the world should be*, relating
each line of each page of each of the far more
than sixteen volumes to the fact that he needed
and wanted and could now only bear to be
alone, with my grandmother having to leave
his food outside the study door, and my father

was surprised once to see how long my grandfather's beard had grown, and my father would often hear him talking to himself, and once my grandfather started shouting so loudly that my grandmother summoned two nurses and, from then on, my grandfather had to take medication which didn't make a great deal of difference, apart from stopping the shouting, because he continued to spend all his time alone.

12.

My grandfather never talked about Auschwitz, and so my father had no option but to plunge into Primo Levi's description of it: the men who steal soup from each other in Auschwitz, the men who pee as they run because they don't have permission to go to the toilet during the working day in Auschwitz, the men who share their bed with other men and sleep with their face next to the feet of those other men and just hope that the latter haven't trodden on the same floor as the men suffering from dysentery, and Primo Levi's ability to bring home to us what it felt like to wake up and get dressed and look out at the snow on the first day of a winter that would last seven months and during which you would work fifteen-hour days with the water up to your knees, carrying sacks of chemical material, all of which helped my father to explain my grandfather's final years. It's easier to blame Auschwitz than to accept what happened to my grandfather. It's easier to blame Auschwitz than to submit oneself to a painful exercise, which is what any child in my father's position would do: seeing my grandfather not as victim, not as a grain of sand crushed by history, which would automatically make my father another grain of sand at the mercy of that same history, and there is nothing easier than to feel almost proud to be that grain of sand, the one that survived the inferno and is here among us to tell the tale, as if my father were my grandfather and my grandfather were Primo Levi and the testimony of my father and my grandfather were the same as Primo Levi's testimony — seeing my grandfather not as a victim, but as a man and a husband and a father, who should be judged just like any other man or husband or father.

13.

The best way to judge my father is to think of him as he was after the fight, when I was thirteen, after he told me about my grandfather and the notebooks and stopped talking about what might happen in a school where there were no Jews. It's odd that he should have spent so much time insisting on this while I was at the previous school, where there was no threat at all, and to have stopped doing so precisely when I started going to the new school, where it wasn't uncommon for me to find a piece of paper in my rucksack bearing a drawing of Hitler. It isn't hard to draw Hitler, and if you were to compare the writing and drawing in the pieces of work we sometimes did in class, you might even find out who the artist was, although it may be that there was more than one artist, because the moustache was sometimes a succession of parallel lines and sometimes a smudge of dots, and the cap might have a short peak or look more like a chef's hat, and the swastika could have thick, painted arms or be more like the stick men drawn by a child, but it didn't matter who the artist or artists were or if the artist or artists knew what the drawings meant because my one question was this: did João in some way know or participate or had he even been the brains behind the plan to give me those drawings?

14.

The eighth grade ended in December, a month in which Porto Alegre is a swamp of heat and humidity, and then it's straight into all the hype about Christmas and New Year, which we usually spent at the beach. I had already begun to drink secretly: on Fridays, my father and mother always went out for the evening together, and I would go to the cupboard, pour myself some whisky and then retreat to my bedroom to watch some trashy TV programme until I fell asleep. It was more or less the same at the beach, except that I had a few summer friends, who at the time had got into the habit of buying *cachaça* and mixing it with soda and orange Fanta, and I can remember walking through the centre of town and seeing Uruguayans playing flutes, stalls selling fritters, or pot-bellied children selling handicrafts, ten o'clock at night and my skin still sticky with salt before going to the cinema to watch a double bill of kung fu and porn, a doorman who never asked how old we were and four hours spent in the dark watching a Chinaman defeating all his opponents one by one followed by a housewife who welcomed with open arms the postman and the gas delivery man and the swimming pool cleaner, the Californian sun and smiling Californian people preaching free love almost half a century after Auschwitz, and the fact that my father had never again mentioned Auschwitz meant that he understood this was something I had to go through alone, me at the cinema with my summer friends who, a few days later, would take me to a brothel where a lady bearing no resemblance to the Californian housewife welcomed us one by one, and I was the last, and the room was lit by a table lamp, and the air was hot and heavy with effort, and the lady asked me to take off my clothes and lie down beside her and she let me cover myself with the thin sheet that my summer friends had already used almost half a century after Auschwitz, and I moved closer to the lady and tried not to think that this was another test, and that I had spent weeks preparing for it, and had drunk four glasses of *cachaça* because of it, and that from then on things might be different.

15.

My father gave me money so that I could go to the brothel. He would join me and my mother at the beach on Fridays. During the week it was just me and her, and on Saturday mornings he liked to fish. I would wake at midday and by the time I found him, he already had a bucket full of catfish, which at best can be made into a rather gritty soup, or kingcroakers that you can cook over the fire, my father and me sitting by the barbecue listening to the crackle and spit from the coal and the firewood while he asked me questions, how things had gone at the brothel, how long I'd spent there, what the lady was like who saw us, and I realised that it didn't matter what questions my father asked, it was the way he asked them, trying to involve himself in my fourteen-year-old life, a moment I stored away perhaps and which is far more evocative than any description of the breeze and the toads croaking and our apparently deserted street, as it always is when I think of that house near the beach.

16.

My relationship with my father changed the day after our fight, in the conversation we had about my grandfather, the notebooks and Auschwitz, during which I realised that I must never again poke fun at or make light of that subject. It was something I should respect as much as he respected my right to study at a new school, and after that tacit agreement the times I spent with him lingered in my memory in a different way: my first year at the new school, my first summer after entering the new school, my visit to the brothel and the night spent sitting by the barbecue and the fact that I felt older and confident enough to answer my father's questions without hesitation and without feeling embarrassed about describing in detail the lobby or the toilets or the room itself and the way I managed to remain calm enough to cover myself with the sheet in front of the lady, and to move closer to her, nails, skin, perfume, and me taking a deep breath and just letting myself go until I fell back exhausted, my mind empty.

17.

If I'd mentioned that conversation by the barbecue when I first learned that my father had Alzheimer's, it's possible that my father would have remembered it all. I could then have continued to use it as a kind of test, asking him to describe other details of the supper, the two of us sitting on plastic chairs, the sink next to the barbecue, the light above the sink, the low brick wall, my mother coming out to us carrying a plate of bread, my father standing with his back to her and her kissing him on the nape of his neck and asking how long before the food would be ready, and that continuous, systematic description could perhaps help reinforce my father's memory, a preparation for the next test, with me asking the same thing again two months later, then six months, then a year, until in subsequent tests his answers began to grow more hesitant and progressively slower, and one day he would look at me as if surprised by what I was saying because it seemed to him a complete novelty or a lie and would remain a novelty or a lie to the end.

18.

My father owned a house in Capão da Canoa, the beach in Rio Grande do Sul with the largest concentration of Jews, including the families of my former classmates, to whom I never spoke again.

19.

In Capão da Canoa I used to go to the cinema, to the amusement arcade, to the bar next to the arcade, where, in the summer between eighth grade and the first year of senior school, I started drinking every night, but none of those places exists today.

20.

Almost all my friends in Capão da Canoa lived on my street, or within a radius of five blocks from my house, and we had met in the way you so often meet when you're a child, a father introduces his son to the son of another father, and the two sons stand side by side not even daring to say hello, and one of the sons is usually brandishing a sword and playing with a castle or a plastic snake that seems to emerge alone from the depths of the sand, and the other son realises that the sword is being used to stop the snake attacking the castle, and, at some point, he makes a gesture or says something as if inviting himself to join in the struggle, and from then on the two will be together every day every summer every year for as long as the house in Capão da Canoa remains standing, but there'll come a time when it will be knocked down and replaced by another building, and the friends' respective parents will move to a different beach, and they'll never hear from each other again.

21.

I've been living in São Paulo for fifteen years now, and it's two years since I got the results of my father's tests and slept in the park not just because I didn't want to think about what I would say to him, but also because I couldn't go home in that state. I've been married three times and was about to separate from my third wife and didn't feel in the least inclined to have a conversation like that with her, because the last thing I needed was to mix up my father's Alzheimer's with our marital problems, at a time when I was doggedly sabotaging any attempt on her part to save me, so there I was lying on a park bench, helpless beneath the dark sky, and that moment was like a summation of everything I had lost since I was fourteen.

22.

Telling this story is like describing the plot of a TV soap, comings and goings, fights and reconciliations for reasons which now seem hard to believe, with me having completed eighth grade thinking that João was responsible for those pictures of Hitler, the drawing itself or the order given for someone else to do it or even a suggestion or a chuckle or a murmur of approval that had the effect of encouraging those who came up with the idea, and at the time I'd already done everything I could to make them stop, and not just by erasing my name chalked on the wall or ignoring them or even smiling benevolently when they mentioned Auschwitz for the first time in the changing room after PE, the first time someone said we'd better make sure it really was water coming out of the showerhead, or when I was in the canteen and they told me not to go too close to the oven, and that would all be quite funny and even a little ridiculous if it weren't for the fact that it was less than a year since your father told you about your grandfather and showed you your grandfather's notebooks, part of them anyway, a page, a line, a sentence was all it took.

23.

It's a little ridiculous to blame the notebooks for my spying on João and spending weeks trying to find some clue that he was the one behind the drawings, a whispered conversation, doodling in class, a couple of occasions when he appeared to hang back at break-time, letting the room empty so that no one would see him slip a piece of paper into my backpack, just as ridiculous as me deciding to respond in kind, by touching him on a nerve as sensitive as the story of my grandfather, another tragedy, another family member, and I'm not proud of the fact that I typed out a few notes at home with precisely that aim, an innocent anonymous font on an innocent anonymous piece of paper that I would put inside João's backpack as soon as I had the chance, just four words, *your mother is dead*, or six, *your mother is six feet under*, or thirteen, *the gravediggers open up your mother's coffin every day and screw her skeleton*.

24.

It isn't the same thing as saying *son-of-a-bitch goy* because, as a curse, that has more to do with the person being attacked than with his mother, the equivalent of calling someone a fag or a queer or a buttfucker, even though the expression *son-of-a-bitch* is stronger than the word *goy*, as was not the case at my previous school. *The gravediggers open up your mother's coffin every day and screw her skeleton* was quite different, and I'm sure it was the first time anyone had said such a thing to João, his shock on discovering that someone was capable of thinking in those terms, and perhaps I should define those terms more clearly, this was someone saying to João that he knew about his mother's death and didn't care about his mother's death and could even make a joke about his mother's death, which was almost tantamount to feeling happy about it.

25.

Was it the same as making a drawing of Hitler? After all, he was the man who ordered Auschwitz to be built and Auschwitz was the place that, according to my father, had destroyed my grandfather, so sending a note alluding to the subject was tantamount to saying that you knew and agreed and were even happy about the destruction of my grandfather, but obviously I still shouldn't have responded as I did. Firstly, because I wasn't sure João was the person behind the drawings, and I still can't be sure even now. I only found one of the drawings on the day when João was the last person to leave the classroom, a day on which I made a point of not getting in his way, going downstairs to the playground and, on my return, immediately hurrying over to look in my backpack as if I wanted to find something, and what I found certainly didn't disappoint me, perhaps the most perfect of the drawings anyone had made during the eighth grade, Hitler mounted on a pig, in fact, I even kept the drawing and admired the details of the scene, the feet, the tail, the Star of David around the pig's snout, and, secondly, because João would be sure to react in the way I expected.

26.

Maybe it was the same as with that classmate in the first week of term, maybe João saw in me an opportunity to assert himself now that he was stronger than me and had more friends and now that I was the only Jew in the building, and it would be easy enough to rally the whole of the eighth grade and the whole school to watch him drag me out into the middle of the playground, where there was a sandpit strategically located, in fact, I think it must be obligatory in any school to have a place where someone can be buried up to the neck, where one can trample and kick the fallen weakling who has long since abandoned any attempt to defend himself, but I wouldn't expect João to react like that. I knew him well enough to know that he wouldn't. I wrote those notes about his mother, one by one, every day, for as long as was necessary, knowing that this was the outer limit, that he wouldn't be prepared to accuse me and fight me over that, because that would mean having to talk about it and say it out loud and let everyone be a witness to it, to the word *mother* that I had never once heard on his lips.

27.

It was his father who told me about João's mother, during the conversation we had at their apartment, on the day when the two of us were left alone watching TV, that programme whose audience was made up of transplants and crutches, and his father asked if I wasn't sorry for what I'd done on his son's birthday. João's mother died before she was forty, when João was little more than a baby, of a cancer that began in her left breast and spread into her bones and chest, and in her final months she stayed at home almost all the time, because her husband preferred that to keeping her in hospital, and after her death João's father moved to a smaller apartment, taking none of the old furniture with him because everything reminded him of her, the bed where she had so often slept before she died, the table where she had so often slept often eaten before she died, the dressing table where she used to sit to put on her make-up and fix her hair and where she had so often asked João's father if she looked pretty or like someone who was dying.

28.

João couldn't say anything about the notes, just as I couldn't say anything about the drawings of Hitler, because he wouldn't want to talk about his mother in public, just as I wouldn't talk about my grandfather. It's easy enough to know this, it's simply a matter of putting yourself in the other person's shoes, João seeing the notes for the first time, and on one of the notes, *the gravediggers open up your mother's coffin every day and screw her skeleton*, I even attempted a drawing showing a raised tombstone, five men dressed in black, four standing and looking down and, inside the grave, a fifth man with the eyes and ears and smile of a devil, and I imagine that João stopped making or commissioning or encouraging whoever it was to produce those drawings of Hitler because of that devil with his legs astride a skeleton, which was all that remained of João's mother, nothing else, just that drawing on a crumpled sheet of paper from an exercise book, no photograph because João's father had decided to throw them all away, no story, and her name never spoken at home, and João's father who never married again and never had a girlfriend and never again considered having more children because all those things would remind him of those final months, João's mother in bed and the painkillers that no longer worked, and I could never forget the expression on his face as he told me that story when I was thirteen, João's father asking me, do you know what it is to feel pain, do you know what it is to spend the whole day screaming in agony, you did what you did to my son and never even thought that there are people who spend months screaming in agony because there isn't enough morphine in the world to relieve their pain, and it was then that João's mother took the initiative, a bottle of painkillers too many, an hour too long left alone, a minute too long before João's father opened the door and spoke to her and realised that something was wrong and then there was nothing more to be done.

A FEW MORE THINGS I KNOW ABOUT MYSELF

1

There are various stages in any diagnosis of Alzheimer's. First there's a straightforward consultation, during which the doctor asks the patient about any memory lapses, if he smokes or drinks, if he's on medication, if he's had any serious illnesses or undergone treatment or surgery in recent years. The doctor takes the patient's pulse, measures his blood pressure, arranges for him to have clinical tests for orientation and language, as well as CT and MRI scans, a dose of thyroid hormones, as well as calcium, phosphorus and vitamin B supplements, he also recommends having PET and SPECT scans, a series of procedures intended to exclude other possible causes of memory lapses, such as stress, dementia, arteriosclerosis, depression or a tumour.

2.

The majority of Alzheimer's patients are aged eighty or over. My father belongs to the three per cent or so aged between sixty and seventy-five, and to the minority whose symptoms were diagnosed at a relatively early stage. At that point, it's possible to slow the pace of the disease with medication, whose technical function is to inhibit acetylcholinesterase, and by maintaining low levels of glycaemia and cholesterol and doing regular exercises for the brain: sudoku, crossword puzzles, asking the patient what he's just read in the newspaper and what he did or didn't do that day.

3.

One often hears of patients making travel plans, reestablishing contact with relatives they've lost touch with, becoming wiser, more adaptable and more tolerant, and being as kind as possible to as many dear friends as possible. The first thing my father did was to arrange matters so that no one would be left with any nasty surprises later on. He updated me on his financial affairs, what property he owned, how the shops were doing in terms of accounts and share price. He also began keeping a kind of record — which, initially, I thought was just another of his memory exercises — the equivalent of a diary of what he ate for breakfast, how often he went to the toilet, who he talked to and what that person said, what they were wearing and what time they left.

4.

It would be pointless trying to imagine his reasoning at the time, and although it all seemed a bit morbid, I couldn't oppose what became my father's principal distraction: hours spent in his study like my grandfather, a project more or less like my grandfather's, a memoir of the places my father had been to, the things he'd seen, the people he'd talked to, a selection of the most important facts drawn from over sixty years of life.

5.

Our family had a house on the beach. It was a big house. Four bedrooms, sitting room, a spacious verandah. A big lawn out front. Most families went to the beach in the morning at around nine o'clock and returned at around one or two o'clock. No one had lunch on the beach. There were no kiosks or people selling popcorn. There was no suntan lotion and the water was much cleaner.

6.

My father has always liked to swim. In the summer, he'd invite me to go for a stroll with him in the late afternoon. It's easy to walk on the firm sand, which feels hard and somehow healthy for your feet, toughening them up. We used to count the number of lifeguard posts, ten there and ten back, then have a swim near where our street met the beach, the warm water and your body being carried gently along by the current, you close your eyes and breathe out when the wave passes. You can feel your muscles when you start swimming crawl or breaststroke, my father breathing more loudly than me, it's very still after a wave has broken and you can see the sand and the light on the lifeguard post opposite the dunes and next to the patch of grass where a thin, weary horse is grazing, my father looks thin and weary too and his wet hair is slick against his head, the skin on his lips puckered, but he's smiling and says in a clear voice that it's been a good day and it's time to go back.

7.

Back at the house, my father has a shower and then I have a shower after him, and when

I come out he's already preparing the fire, and I sit down beside him and that's when we have our chat by the barbecue: he starts telling me about his technique of heating up the coals from underneath, like a pyramid in which, in the midst of all that blackness, you can make out a few glowing red spots that gradually multiply. At that point you add more coal and expose the centre which is now the kind of red-hot heat that won't flare up when any fat drips onto it, and then he starts talking about the car and the road and the unpaved street, about the faulty electricity meter on the wall and the guttering that needs mending, and that's when he asks about the brothel, and I tell him everything and I can see the expression of relief on his face, the look of trust that instantly defuses all the doubt and anxiety that had been there at the start, because I'd never known my father talk so much about so many things as on that night.

8.

After I answer his questions about the brothel, my father tells me that it had been pretty much like that in his day too, a lady he never saw again and whose name he couldn't remember.

9.

My father told me about the women he'd gone out with before he met my mother, one was studying architecture and another was from a family who lived close by, but he didn't describe what they looked like, their hair, skin, height, and as far as I know he never spoke to any of them again.

10.

My father told me that this was a special time for me. Then he asked about senior school and if I'd given any thought to what I'd like to study at university, but that I shouldn't be in a hurry and he would support me in whatever choice I made, and that I should focus on what I really wanted to study and not worry about money or about whether the entrance exam was easy or difficult or about what characters in TV soaps or in the ads had to say.

11.

It's a good moment to start thinking about these decisions, he said. My father was worried because I would be changing schools for a second time. It was the end of the second semester of the eighth grade, heralding another period of interviews, evaluations and tests. I could have gone to a school run by Marists, Baptists, Buddhists, Jesuits, Pentecostalists or Umbandistas, Mormons or Seventh-Day Adventists, but at that point my father wasn't interested in the school's religious orientation or teaching methods. This time, he wanted to know why I was so keen to change schools yet again. It was easy enough to come up with the excuses he wanted to hear, telling him that the teachers were weak and favoured rote learning, that the head teacher was too rigid and that I didn't really hit it off with my classmates, because this was better than telling him about the notes and the drawings, about João's mother and my grandfather.

12.

To talk about João's mother and about my grandfather today is to return to all the references I absorbed over the years, the films, the photographs, the documents, the first time I read *If This Is a Man* and felt there was really nothing more to be said on the subject. I don't know how many of those who did write about it had read the book, but I doubt that any of those texts contains anything that Primo Levi had not said already. Adorno wrote that there could be no more poetry after Auschwitz, Yehuda Amichai wrote that there could be no more theology after Auschwitz, Hannah Arendt wrote that Auschwitz revealed the existence of a particular kind of evil, and then there are the books by Bruno Bettelheim, Victor Klemperer, Viktor Frankl, Paul Celan, Aharon Appelfeld, Ruth Klüger, Anne Frank, Elie Wiesel, Imre Kertész, Art Spiegelman and so many, many others, but in a way they couldn't go beyond what Primo Levi says about his companions in the hut, those who stood in the same line, those who shared the same mug, those who set off into the dark night of 1945 where more than twenty thousand people disappeared without trace on the day before the camp was liberated.

13.

To talk about João's mother and about my grandfather today is to distort the story by imposing on it an entirely phoney logic, rhetoric and rhythm, like trying to impress an audience by leaving the cruellest, most shocking, most violent scenes until last, the ones that arouse the strongest feelings of identification and pity just before the moment of catharsis, and with time and experience and repeated readings of *If This Is a Man* you learn to do that really well and to reproduce those feelings without really suffering, because you exhaust that suffering the first or second or third time you describe the atrocities, using the grave voice you've learned to put on when you say that a million and a half adults arrived at Auschwitz, and started to work and sleep and eat under the camp's regime, and it's worth adding that within a few months those adults weighed something like fifty kilos, or forty, or thirty, and that the camp officials took each and every one of those million and a half adults weighing thirty kilos, and escorted each and every one of those million and a half adults weighing thirty kilos, and opened the door of the gas chamber to each and every one of those million and a half adults weighing thirty kilos, and turned the tap that filled the chamber with gas where each and every one of those million and a half adults was waiting, you can repeat this ad nauseam because you're never going to feel what you felt when you were fourteen, when you came home after writing the last of those notes about João's mother and receiving the last of the notes containing a drawing of Hitler, and went into your room and sat down on the bed and for the first time had some notion of what it all meant.

14.

I spent the second semester of the eighth grade at home, not seeing a single friend at the weekend, and although my father never said anything I think he knew about the bottles of whisky in the cupboard: he couldn't fail to notice the level slowly going down, a little lower on Friday, still lower on Saturday, and sometimes during the week as well, and it would be somewhat ridiculous to say that I was doing this only because of João's mother and my grandfather, although there's no denying their influence on my behaviour, me sitting on the bed in my room, knowing I would never again write those notes and never again receive one, and that I would never again speak to João and he would never again speak to me, and that in some way this was one effect of what had happened to his mother and to my grandfather.

15.

Family — group of people who share the house with the man and in doing so crown his desire for continuity and a loving, giving relationship, confirming the good luck he has always enjoyed in life. When living with him the other family members take care that their ideas or attitudes are never incompatible with his, this includes the observance of the most rigorous hygiene procedures in the upkeep of the house and in items such as food and clothing, which includes taking care over food-stuffs and the hygienic treatment of clothing using for the purpose products such as soap and fabric conditioner as well as detergent for the household china and disinfectant for the floor, using a mop and various cloths to remove dust. The family members should also observe the rules of communal living insofar as it affects the man's personality, respecting him in his moments of strength and weakness and ensuring that his wishes are respected whenever he chooses to remain alone in his study. The family never disturbs him when he is alone in his study. The family must respect his right, which he can exercise on any day and at any hour and without permission or prior warning, to remain for as long as he likes alone in his study.

16.

My grandfather lost a brother in Auschwitz, and another brother in Auschwitz, and a third brother in Auschwitz, and his father and his mother in Auschwitz, and his girlfriend of the time in Auschwitz, and at least one cousin and one aunt in Auschwitz, and who knows how many friends in Auschwitz, how many neighbours, how many work colleagues, how many people he would have been quite close to had he not been the only one to survive and set off on a boat for Brazil and spend the rest of his life without ever mentioning any of their names.

17.

At fourteen I sat down on the bed with the bottle of whisky I'd taken from the cupboard knowing that my grandfather had never stopped thinking about Auschwitz. My grandfather went out to buy bread and the newspaper: Auschwitz. My grandfather said good morning to my grandmother: Auschwitz. My grandfather shut himself up in his study knowing that my father was on the other side of the door, his son gaining his adult teeth and growing slightly taller, and you could be there with him when he uses a new word and ends a sentence in a different way, and laughs at something you weren't expecting him to understand at his age, and looks at you and you see his face when he's eight and ten and fourteen, but you're not there because time has sped past and you've never known a single moment when you did anything but think about all those names, about each and every one of the people who were with you in the train and in the hut and at the work camp and at every moment during the time you spent in Auschwitz, apart from the day when you were freed.

18.

Would it make any difference if I were to explain how each and every one of my grandfather's relatives died? Would anyone be particularly moved if his brother, another brother, a third brother, his father and mother, his girlfriend and at least one cousin and one aunt, and who knows how many friends and neighbours and work colleagues and people he was quite close to, if each and every one of them had suffered a more or less natural death in Auschwitz, in the hospital or in the work camps, or if they had been sent to the gas chamber, been given a hanger for their clothes and, while they waited for what they thought would be a hot shower, listened to the music that the guards ordered to be played, and meanwhile the pellets of hydrogen cyanide were exposed to the air to release a gas, and that gas was breathed in, it entered the bloodstream, and

149

some people were in such agony they hurled themselves against the walls in despair, and this lasted until all of them finally fell and were dragged outside and placed on an operating table where the bodies were sliced open, the fat cut out, the teeth extracted, the eyes removed, and each and every organ placed in separate receptacles, liver, kidney, pancreas, stomach, lungs, heart, so that all that remained was the carcass and the bones, and the carcass and the bones were thrown into pits, a million and a half holes dug and filled with skeletons that had once been nameless adults weighing thirty kilos?

19.

Or if my grandfather's brother, another brother and a third brother and his father and mother, and his girlfriend, and at least one cousin and one aunt, and who knows how many friends and neighbours and work colleagues and people he was quite close to, if each of them had been used for the scientific experiments they say were carried out in Auschwitz, deliberate exposure to chlorine gas or mustard gas, deliberate infection with hepatitis and malaria, induced hypothermia in a tank of freezing water with a probe stuck up their rectum, a doctor who injected ink to see if the patient's eyes would change colour, a doctor who sewed two twins together, a doctor who sewed up a woman's belly with a cat inside, a group of twenty-three doctors who repeatedly raped a woman whose eyes had been injected with colouring and whose bloodstream had been infected with malaria and hepatitis and tetanus, a woman who weighed only thirty kilos, who had previously been immersed in a tank of water and sulphuric acid at freezing temperatures with a probe stuck up her rectum and a live cat sewn inside her belly, her teeth extracted so that she couldn't bite the doctors, her fat removed to be turned into soap, her organs stored for future use, liver, kidney, pancreas, stomach, lungs, heart, appendix, trachea, muscles, tendons, ganglia, nails, hair, skin, gums, her bones thrown into a pit with another million and a half skeletons who were once adults who had been repeatedly raped and dissected and given electric shocks and doused in kerosene ready to be thrown on the fire beneath the Auschwitz sky?

20.

Would it make any difference if the things I'm describing are still true more than half a century after Auschwitz, when no one can bear to hear about it any more, when even to me it seems old-fashioned to write about it, or are those things only of importance to me because of the implications they had for the lives of all those around me?

21.

I'm forty now and, two years ago, I got drunk and slept on a park bench on the day I found out about my father's Alzheimer's. I didn't want my third wife to see me in that state and ask questions because then the only way of escaping another quarrel and possibly the final act of my third marriage would be to tell her about my visit to the doctor that afternoon, and give her the results of my father's tests, and allow her to see my reaction when I spoke about the diagnosis, and perhaps tell her everything I knew about my father and everything I knew about my grandfather and, consequently, everything I knew about me.

22.

My grandfather died on a Sunday, at around seven o'clock in the morning, when all the doctors are at home and the hospital emergency services are in the hands of interns or duty doctors on the red-eye shift. On a Sunday it's harder to deal with the practical side of any death: the bureaucracy involved in getting the body released, telling all your friends, contacting the cemetery, getting a death notice printed in the newspaper.

23.

I don't know if my father went to the funeral. I don't know how long it took him to make the connection between my grandfather's death and Auschwitz, if he did so on that very day, at that very moment, or if this only became clear when he read my grandfather's notebooks, and there would inevitably have been a delay between their discovery and the delivery of the translation that my father commissioned without telling my grandmother. I don't know who did the translation, I don't know how my father paid them, I don't know if he asked the translator to keep quiet about it, if he made it clear to the translator that he or she should make no comment on what the notebooks contained, because up until then my father had no idea what my grandfather had written in those

sixteen volumes without ever once mentioning the relatives he saw die, and it's possible
that he may have seen each and every one of
them die, the last breath, the wide, lifeless
eyes of his brother, another brother, a third
brother, of his father and mother, of his
girlfriend and his cousin and his aunt and
who knows how many friends and neighbours
and work colleagues and people he was quite
close to, my father making it clear to the
translator that he didn't want him to make
any comment on any such scenes because
none could justify the scene of my grandfather lying dead at seven o'clock on a
Sunday morning.

24.

When you're fourteen, it's highly unlikely
that you would wake up at seven in the
morning with the house still in silence and
instantly slip out of bed and go to the
bathroom and then to the kitchen to get
something from the fridge, that would only
make sense if you'd been woken by a dream
or a presentiment or a noise, and whenever
my father talked about Auschwitz I think he
was remembering precisely that day, my
father opening his eyes (Auschwitz) and

jumping out of bed (Auschwitz) and opening the door of his room (Auschwitz) and hesitating when he remembered the study where my grandfather had spent that night and every night since he had finally given up his battle with those memories.

25.

When I was fourteen I drank whisky alone in my room because I had come face to face with those memories too. They were in the drawings of Hitler, in the notes I wrote about João's mother, in the certainty that because of them I could never again be João's friend and would change schools and meet other people and get on with my life never knowing what became of João, if he was alive (Auschwitz), if he was still living in Porto Alegre (Auschwitz), if he had children (Auschwitz), if he became a doctor or a lawyer or a bus conductor (Auschwitz), if even once during those more than twenty years he realised that making a drawing of Auschwitz was the same as making a drawing of his mother's illness, because Auschwitz was for my grandfather what that illness was for his mother, and my grandfather's story and his mother's story were the same.

26.

A story that ends and begins with my father emerging, frightened, from his room next to my grandmother's, and I don't know if my grandmother was sleeping or if she had woken up as well, my grandmother alone in her bed, and now they both know they have to go forward, step by step along the corridor, the silence of the house and the world on a Sunday morning on which the only thing that had happened was that bang, a sound my father never stopped hearing, it was there between the lines of all our conversations about my grandfather, every time my father uttered that word, that short, sharp bang was there in every syllable of that word, *Auschwitz*, my father walking over to the study door, which was locked, because my grandfather made sure of that, making it difficult for someone to open the door because that way he would gain a minute or five or ten or half an hour until they found a way of forcing the lock or kicking in the wooden panels, and with each kick my father somehow knew what he would find on the other side, because he had knocked on the door and called my grandfather and shouted several times and my grandfather couldn't possibly be sleeping or simply waiting for the door to be broken down, and the short, sharp bang (Auschwitz) that came from the study (Auschwitz) which my father finally managed to enter (Auschwitz) with the help of a crowbar (Auschwitz) would inevitably be what my father had imagined it would be (Auschwitz), a fact he confirmed when he saw, through the crack in the door, my grandfather's white hair and his head, arms, trunk and whole body slumped across the desk.

NOTES (2)

You just have to go on the Internet to read that the fifty-two ovens in Auschwitz wouldn't have been large enough to burn four thousand seven hundred and fifty-six bodies a day, the average needed to achieve the total number of deaths in the official statistics.

There are endless texts stating that the gas chambers could not possibly have worked, because the gas released by the particles of hydrogen cyanide would have dispersed and because of the difficulty of fitting that number of people into one of those compartments without arousing their suspicions. The gas would kill the guards when they went into the chamber after the executions. Even if they had installed some miraculous ventilation system that could eliminate any risk of contact with the respiratory system, even if the guards wore masks, which weren't one hundred per cent effective at the time anyway, you would still have to extract every single particle and pump it out into the air, where, of course, it would have killed anyone who happened to be standing downwind — guards, officials, officers.

Just one click and you'll find someone

161

telling you that there are no photos or architectural plans of the gas chambers. That there was no reason to kill the prisoners, who were working for the Germans. That there was no reason to reduce the capacity of the camps, which produced coal, synthetic rubber, chemical components, weapons and fuel, and thus boosted the country's economy, benefiting companies such as BMW, Daimler-Benz, the Deutsche Bank, Siemens and Volkswagen.

I've read that not only Jews died of starvation, but a large portion of the German population. That the problem isn't the number of deaths, but whether those deaths were brought about deliberately, and not a single document has been found containing explicit orders to carry out the final solution, nor a single piece of testimony from a Nazi source made with a lawyer present and under oath, something that is highly unlikely if, as is alleged, it was a decision made at the top and passed down to generals, colonels, majors, lieutenants, sergeants, corporals and privates, as well as to all the civil servants and police involved in the machinery of extermination.

I've read and heard a lot of things along those lines, as well as each and every one of the counter-arguments, and I could talk for hours on the subject because there are people who have devoted their whole lives to formulating these questions and answers, but what matters here isn't whether or not the number of deaths was exaggerated. Or if the deaths did or didn't happen exactly as described in the official version. Or if what some people term an industry has since grown up based on that version. Or if what those people call an industry is used now to justify any kind of active oppression which, with a little rhetorical and moral flexibility, can then be compared to the oppression suffered during the Second World War.

What matters here, regardless of the gravity of the subject — because if Auschwitz had killed only one person on the grounds of ethnicity or religious belief, the mere existence of such a place would be just as appalling — what matters is that any lie or imprecision, however small or large, would make no difference to my father, because for him Auschwitz was never a place, a historical fact or an ethnic debate, but a concept in which one believes or ceases to believe simply because one chooses to.

NOTES (3)

My father doesn't have the same name as my grandfather. I don't have the same name as my father. There are a whole series of other things I didn't inherit from him either: hair, nose, handwriting. I also don't do complicated mental arithmetic or enjoy listening to the radio in the morning, the same programme every day, a battery radio with the volume turned down low and a presenter who talks about the violence and the traffic and the thieves currently in parliament while my father eats bread and a slice of cheese and makes a chewing noise that has annoyed my mother for more than forty years, and for a good part of the morning she complains because he hasn't cleared the table and didn't pick up the phone and hasn't answered a single question she's asked him in those same more than forty years, and by about ten or eleven they're talking normally again and planning a journey to some country where he can spend at least one afternoon safely ensconced in shops that sell electronic equipment while she buys clothes and presents and he complains because you could fill a whole cargo terminal with all those packages for people no one has ever even heard of.

From my father I inherited the colour of his eyes (brown and slightly yellow on very bright days), the reading habit (fiction in my case, non-fiction in his), a few favourite foods (barbecued meat, melted cheese, rice mixed with gravy and egg yolk). I'm stubborn like him too. Learning that he had Alzheimer's was the only moment in my forty years when I really thought about stubbornness, if you can call it that, and if you can credit it with the fact that I've reached the age of forty having told my father most of my stories, every decision I made about what seemed important at the time, renting an apartment, choosing a profession, changing careers and cities, the beginning and end of two marriages, the books I've written and the things I've most enjoyed and whatever else I can fit into a weekly phone call to Porto Alegre summarising what I believe he needs to know, at least in the sense of distracting him and distracting myself so that neither of us will need to say anything about the fact that from then on that's pretty much how it will be, a half-hour chat each week and a couple of visits a year, when we'll spend a brief, pleasant day pretending that time hasn't passed, and that it will always be possible for me to continue

168

hiding from him my most important secret, which in some way has always defined who I am, and in some way too can only be explained by a concept — a truth or a lie or both things, depending on how you react to a scene like that of my grandfather slumped over his desk.

THE FALL

1.

My favourite drink used to be whisky. At one time it was vodka. And I went through a lot of different cocktail phases: Bloody Mary, dry Martini, mojito. Over the years, I developed a particular intolerance for champagne. I like beer, but not in large quantities. I was never keen on liqueurs. The same goes for any drink that tastes like syrup, Campari or Underberg for example, or drinks made from aniseed: I have a particular intolerance for anything that tastes of aniseed.

2.

Wine is good. I haven't drunk Steinhäger in ages. I'm not a fan of straight rum. And I rarely drink *cachaça*. I like cognac. Gin. Bourbon. Pisco. Punch. Sangria. Sake. Tequila. Port wine. Single malt. Hi-fi. Mint julep. Sea breeze. White Russian. B52. Jumping monkey. Alexander. Sex on the beach. Piña colada.

3.

The first sign that you have a drink problem is the fact that half of your conversations revolve around the subject, and ninety per cent of those conversations revolve around the fact that you no longer drink as much as you did, and you can spend years saying that, yes, you did go through a really rough patch but you've sorted yourself out now and you go to bed early and you've taken up sport, and how dangerous it is to drive around the way you used to do, and you really thought you'd never reach forty if you carried on like that, and you say this in the same tone of voice as those people who always have some tale to tell about an incident in a bathroom or in the gutter or at a birthday party where you astonished everyone by walking through a glass door and emerging with just a tiny cut on your nose, but when you've been married three times and are just about to leave your third wife it's really not that funny any more.

4.

I woke up with a stiff neck and in broad daylight. It wasn't until after seven o'clock that I realised I'd spent the whole night in the park. The envelope containing the results of my father's tests was still intact, and at a moment like that you don't think about turning over and sleeping a little longer or getting up and heading for a newspaper stand or a café where you can order a coffee and give instructions on when exactly your toast should be removed from the grill. You don't think about anything, you just need to carry out those tasks one by one, each bite, each sip, taking care not to burn your tongue, the visit to the toilet to wash your face, the bill paid with your debit card, and two years later I know that the instant I opened my eyes that day things had already changed, it was the first morning I'd woken up with an awareness that I had responsibilities, how my father would spend his days and who would look after him.

5.

My father started writing his memoirs immediately after finding out that he had Alzheimer's. I never asked him why, not just because I didn't want to interfere in such a healthy activity for someone in his position, but because, given the way he wrote and what he wrote, its significance was fairly obvious.

6.

I had already noticed her at the beach. I asked her: doesn't your family usually holiday in Capão? Where are you staying? Where do you sit on the beach? I enjoy swimming in the sea and in the heated pool too. At the same time, I was waiting for the next piece of music to begin. When it did I would ask her to dance. It was dark in the hall. In the far corner, the organisers had hung a spinning, glittering globe. I knew half the people there. They knew me too, I think. Everyone was looking at me. Men had to wear a tie in those days. There wasn't a man in the room who wasn't wearing a tie.

7.

Perhaps my father thought of it as a kind of exercise for the brain, the equivalent of a crossword, each sentence helping to prolong his memory of things, like taking notes in class which, when you study them later, become everything the teacher said, but I don't really believe that. That's no reason to write a book of memoirs, knowing that in the future an illness will prevent you reading it, unless you've reached the point my grandfather reached when he wrote his.

8.

My father only spoke about my grandfather's death once, after the fight we had when I was thirteen, but that was enough for me to imagine what it must have been like for him to open that study door when he was fourteen, the moment before he took a step and went over to the desk. I never asked him what was on the desk, papers, pens, or if my grandfather had left a note or taken the trouble to cover the carpet with something or to position himself so that his blood wouldn't spatter the wall, and if they had to get a decorator in afterwards and agree a price and pretend that the stain had been caused by an accident at a party, someone tripping and spilling their glass of wine, and that no one was hurt or found their life changed for ever.

9.

I imagine my father when he was fourteen, sixteen, eighteen, his days divided between school and the shop, the silent suppers with my grandmother, his course in business studies, a few friends, a few girlfriends, and the dance where he met my mother. As he got to know my mother better, I can't believe that the Sunday morning when my grandfather died didn't cast a shadow over their relationship. Not just in the way one would expect, the inevitability of that ending when one considers the life my grandfather had known, his memoirs, and forgive me for returning yet again to the subject and mentioning that word *Auschwitz* yet again, and yet again evoking its meaning, but also as regards their future together.

10.

Forgive me if I say again that Auschwitz helps to justify what my grandfather did, if I find it easier to blame Auschwitz than to accept what my grandfather did, if I feel more comfortable continuing to list the horrors of Auschwitz, because I have a sense that everyone's rather tired of hearing about that, and the number of Auschwitz survivors who ended up exactly like Primo Levi and my grandfather, I once read a long report on the subject, someone in Mexico, someone in Switzerland, in Canada, in South Africa, and in Israel, a brotherhood of ninety-year-old gentlemen who lived alone in a room in some boarding house, an epidemic of ninety-year-old gentlemen in a city and in a country and in a world where they knew no one and where no one remembered anything any more, and forgive me if thinking about this is simpler than indulging in an obvious exercise: imagining that my grandfather didn't do what he did just because of Primo Levi and those other gentlemen, or because he was like Primo Levi and those other gentlemen, or because he didn't know how to avoid ending up like them, but for some reason closely bound up with my father.

11.

In thirty years' time it will be almost impossible to find anyone who was imprisoned in Auschwitz.

12.

In sixty years' time it will be very hard to find the son of anyone who was imprisoned in Auschwitz.

13.

In three or four generations the name Auschwitz will have about as much importance as the names Majdanek, Sobibor and Belzec have today.

14.

Does anyone remember now whether it was eighty or eighty thousand people who died in Majdanek, two hundred or two hundred thousand in Sobibor, five hundred or five hundred thousand in Belzec? Does it make any difference thinking in numerical terms, about the fact that Auschwitz and the other camps modelled on Auschwitz killed nearly six million Jews? Did it matter to my father that not only six million Jews were killed, but twenty million other people, if you include Gypsies, Slavs, homosexuals, the physically and mentally handicapped, common criminals, prisoners of war, Muslims, atheists, and Jehovah's Witnesses? Or that it wasn't in fact just twenty million, but seventy million if you take into account all the other war casualties: the English, Russian, French, Polish, Chinese, American, Greek, Belgian, Spanish, Ukrainian and Swedish, and, yes, even the Japanese, Italians and Germans who died, all of whose deaths were a direct and indirect consequence of the actions of those who built Auschwitz? What did any of that mean to my father? Did it justify the fact that my grandfather did what he did without for a moment considering him or what his life would be like from then on, the burden he would have to carry with him ever after?

15.

My father grew up as my grandfather's son, and I won't bother repeating the arguments offered by medicine and psychology and culture that prove how harmful such a model can be, the father figure who did what he did, who discarded his son in the way he did, and I imagine how even the simplest of things must have weighed on my father, school and the shop, the silent suppers with my grandmother, his course in business studies, a few friends, a few girlfriends and the dance where he met my mother, the weight of leaving that dance thinking about her, the first time he phoned her and arranged to go to the cinema and picked her up at her house and held her hand and met her family and gradually grew close enough to discuss the possibility of me being born of that union a few years later.

16.

I imagine what my father felt when he was at the hospital, when my mother was in labour, if it was any different for him than for any other father, if he had to make a special effort to play the role, put on the words and the gestures, the pretence at commitment and support, the external displays of affection, the external embraces, the external smile, not to mention the fact that he was perhaps thinking about my grandfather and waking each day with the fear that he might repeat what my grandfather had done, and looking at me each day thinking that I might become what he was if he became what my grandfather was.

17.

I have been the person I am from very early on, and I wonder if it makes any sense to keep mentioning Auschwitz in this story. But if it doesn't make any sense to blame Auschwitz for what happened to my grandfather and consequently what happened to my father, how can I make a connection between all of that and the fact that I never again spoke to João? Less than a year after we became friends, I was capable of writing him a note about his mother's death, and of using his mother's death to avoid having a physical confrontation with him, because having a physical confrontation would be yet another attack on his integrity, a repetition of what I did on his birthday, because in a fight you don't think so very differently from when you allow someone to fall flat on his back while the other guests are all singing 'Happy Birthday', the intention is the same, the result is the same if all goes to plan, if I managed to hit him during the fight, if in front of the whole of the eighth grade I managed to land a punch on him or knock him down and kick and stamp and spit in his face to the point where he would never get up again.

18.

I wrote my last note about the death of João's mother, and went home and stole the bottle of whisky from the cupboard, and locked myself in my room and sat on the bed, and took a deep breath before taking my first swallow, knowing that I would never again say so much as hello to João. I would walk down the corridors averting my face from his, and for the rest of my life I would never again have a conversation in which I mentioned his name, because that would be a reminder of what I was capable of doing to him not just once but over and over again. How could the impact of that discovery be mitigated or justified by what I had recently learned about Auschwitz? Because even though Auschwitz was considered to be the greatest tragedy of the twentieth century, and that includes the millions of people who have died in wars and massacres and under all kinds of regimes, a mere bureaucratic statistical account of the victims who disappeared all that time ago, even my grandfather, and even my father indirectly, not one of those victims was anywhere near as important to me as João was when I was fourteen.

19.

It was around then that I started to drink, and I could even list the things I ruined because of that in the years that followed. A job, because I couldn't wake up early enough. A car, which I wrote off in an accident and in which the guy I was giving a lift to fractured his arm. My first two marriages, which in one way or another ended because of that.

20.

My first wife was from Porto Alegre, and we lived in her apartment before I moved to São Paulo. I hadn't even finished my journalism degree when I received an invitation to work for a magazine. She was a psychologist and had already built up a practice and, right from the start, we knew that it was highly unlikely that she would move to São Paulo, as unlikely as my return to a city where I would soon have no friends and nothing to do, and then it was just a matter of time before I began to rehearse in my head the inevitable conversation, the holiday weekend when I grew tired of hiding the fact that I'd already met the woman who would become my second wife.

21.

On that holiday weekend I told her everything, immediately after I woke up, in Porto Alegre. I was due to go back to São Paulo that evening. On holidays we spent the mornings in bed. My first wife used to read the newspaper with me. She thought that because I was a journalist I would enjoy discussing the different sections, the opinion pieces and the classifieds. We used to have lunch at home, she liked cooking, and my flight was nearly always in the late afternoon, because the next day I had to be at work, and at around five o'clock, she would take me to the airport and I always used to imagine what the last time would be like, if she would still give me a lift, if there would be a farewell embrace or kiss, in the lobby or next to the sign for domestic flights, or if I would leave without looking back and take the stairs so as to reach the street more quickly and hail a taxi while she stared at the closed door and the empty apartment and the unmade bed and only then would she shrink into herself and take a deep breath and close her eyes and then somehow subside into an agony that overwhelmed every part of her body.

22.

I broke the news to her as objectively as I could, and although I spoke about sadness and sorrow and guilt, what I remember most vividly is a shameful feeling of relief, and of all the things I learned from the years I spent with my first wife, that is, the lessons that a first relationship always teaches you, the first time a woman says she loves you, the first time you accept that and how you deal with it, and how you cope with the endless problems it brings, the way you speak, the way you dress, how selfish, inconsiderate, lying and manipulative you are, how unfaithful, immature and untrustworthy you are, both emotionally and as regards ordinary domestic matters, all of which only compounds the sense of oppression felt by your partner, in short, of all the things I learned in those years when I was ceaselessly accused and judged and condemned by my first wife, for being the way I was and always would be because of my lack of effort and commitment to her, the most important thing is the certainty that I made the right decision on that holiday morning.

23.

With my second wife it was quite different, and not only because she was, of course, a different person — the mere fact that she'd been married before and was nearly thirty when I met her and wasn't a psychologist and therefore didn't use jargon or tricks in any of the conversations we had in the six years we spent together was already a great advantage — but also because I had changed too: no one emerges unscathed from a break-up, and no one gets married again without having some idea of what he or she is or isn't prepared to accept. It's easier to impose limits then, and a tacit or overt agreement is enough for you not to have to hide certain of your habits, like going alone to places frequented by other people on their own, where all you have to do is say hello, all you have to do is come up with an excuse for being there, standing at the bar opposite a mirrored wall full of coloured bottles, and then how can you possibly go home that night or the following day, and this continues for months and years, you entering the apartment and looking at your second wife, barely able to believe she can be so understanding.

24.

The problem with my second marriage wasn't reaching that agreement, largely because my second wife enjoyed equal freedom, the banal result being that in those six years I must have been with any number of other women, and she must have been with any number of other men, and within those rules it was all done as discreetly and respectfully as possible. The problem with my second marriage was that, despite the absence of quarrels, despite the mutual cooperation and my second wife's extreme generosity and the degree to which that helped her keep hanging on in the hope that I would change, for the day when I would finally get my act together, the historic day when I wouldn't simply allow myself to succumb yet again, my clothes and my body exuding alcohol, the thing I insisted on becoming on those occasions, try to get up and talk and keep looking straight ahead, and just once not end the night in the same way, in the same state and proffering the same excuses when you get home, despite all that, I was never in love with her. My second wife knew this. In fact, she always knew, and she stood it for as long as she could until she finally gave up and met someone else and decided to move on, and I never again heard anything more about her.

25.

According to the World Health Organization, alcoholism causes physical, spiritual and mental harm. Studies have been made that establish safe limits for consumption, allowing for variables of tolerance and dependency according to gender, weight, race and the cultural context in which the patient lives, but it's easy enough to see how well someone does or doesn't fit the model. I read a book once that described depression as the inability to feel affection, and perhaps there's a similar analogy to be made with drink. Not in an organic, chemical sense, but in the sense that you know exactly what will happen each time you stand leaning at one of those colourful bars, each time you get into a car or enter an apartment or a toilet with a person who, if she's lucky, will get a smile from you or a whisper or a groan that is a mixture of tiredness and sadness for something that will be over in two minutes, and while I managed to conceal all this from my first wife, because most of the time I was in São Paulo and she was in Porto Alegre, from then on the story changes: my second wife who left me because of that, my third wife who I met because of that, a relationship which, right from the start, circled endlessly around the subject.

26.

That's what I was thinking about when I got the results of my father's tests. The day I met my third wife. The day I had my first serious conversation with her on the subject. The day

I realised that she wasn't prepared to make any concessions and how, throughout our time together, throughout our marriage, the subject of my drinking was never far away, it was in fact the sole cause of the quarrels, the initial crises, the initial threats, the many occasions on which she spent hours waiting up for me so that we could try and do what we always did throughout that time, the same discussions lasting into the early hours, saying and doing the same things out of weakness or compulsion.

27.

My third wife and I had the last of those early-morning discussions a few days before I got the results of my father's tests. I slept in the park almost by chance really, because I could easily have booked myself into a hotel or even gone home. Given the results of those tests, she would perhaps not have told me off for getting drunk again, but I didn't want her to see me like that because there comes a point when you feel ashamed of the shame she must feel for you, and when you're exhausted and in no condition for an encounter that might seal the fate that was always looming on the horizon, going under alone, ending up alone, all you can do is play for time.

28.

As arranged with the doctor, I received the results by email, in São Paulo. I opened the document and printed it out. Right from the start, I knew I would have to go to Porto Alegre. I couldn't give my father the news over the phone, and so before I fell asleep in the park I'd already bought my plane ticket. I'd already spoken to my third wife about the trip, and had already been suitably succinct and grave when I lied to her about the doctor wanting to see me, saying that he preferred not to go into greater detail until he'd spoken to me in person, and telling her that we would talk when I got back and I could then think about what to do regarding that most recent early-morning argument, assuming I had anything new to say on the subject, and so it was, going through the various procedures at the airport one by one, checking in, waiting, boarding, so it was that this whole long story began to move towards its end.

29.

Telling the story of your life from when you were fourteen involves, I repeat, accepting that facts — even gratuitous facts or facts that, due to circumstance, defy all logic

— can nevertheless be linked together as cause and effect. As if by talking about João and about the last time we spoke, shortly before the end of eighth grade, I were looking for the origin of what happened on that trip to Porto Alegre, almost three decades later. At fourteen, I sat down on my bed, alone in my room, with a bottle of whisky beside me, my first drink after ceasing to be João's friend, aware of the pain I had caused my best friend and of the pain he had caused me, and I could easily have said that I never again felt like that. That, in terms of my age, and the importance friendship has for someone of that age, too young to have learned to take an ironic or sceptical view of endings and deaths and the routine that inevitably engulfs all things, in those terms I felt something that I would only begin to feel again when I boarded that plane, after reading the results of my father's tests, after that last argument with my third wife.

30.

I've always hated planes. I loathe everything to do with flying: the taxi to the airport, the zigzag queues, the trays for any metal objects, the boarding tunnel, the smell of jet fuel. I spend days worrying about that moment when your seat suddenly feels light and when the shaking diminishes as the plane gains altitude, and the continuous futile throb of the engines that always seem to be working at full throttle, and the sandwich and the napkin and the plastic and the gassy drinks, and the clothes worn by the cabin crew, and the conversations about sales figures between executives from provincial cities, and the window and the threads of water that turn into a storm on the eternal night during which you're on board that box of compressed air, me plunging through space towards the dark empty countryside where not even my teeth will be identifiable, five hundred metres, two hundred metres, at a speed impossible to imagine the instant before you close your eyes in readiness for the impact and the explosion.

31.

I arrive at Porto Alegre airport alone. My parents no longer live in the same part of town as when I was fourteen. The streets are all tarmacked, and the city is busier, and the cars are new and the people are different and I know hardly any of the shops and bars and restaurants and pharmacies and buildings that seemed to have sprung up at an unstoppable, predatory rate.

32.

I rang the entryphone. The lobby is furnished with rugs and a leather sofa. I hadn't said I was coming, and my mother was waiting for me when the lift door opened. She'd gone with my father to see the doctor and suspected that the doctor would get in touch with me about the tests if anything was wrong, and why else would I be in Porto Alegre at that hour of the day, the sun in Porto Alegre isn't the same as when I was fourteen, the air in Porto Alegre isn't the same, the sound of the cars and the birds and the children playing behind a wall somewhere despite the news I had to give to my father and which was there on my mother's face the moment she saw me.

33.

My mother took a step back and I was afraid she might fall, or was on the verge of fainting, because she realised that this was the final moment before everything else began to collapse, her years at my father's side, the person she had been at my father's side, and it's that kind of reaction I'm talking about, the reaction of someone who really cares about another person, whether that person is their father or their best friend or their first or second or third wife, the way you feel and express yourself regardless of the shouting and the possibility that your third wife is about to leave you, the conversation she and I had after that last early-morning argument, when we finally reached our limit, had gone as far as we were capable of going, the plea from my third wife that marked perhaps the final act of my marriage.

34.

The plea, the same one I'd been hearing since I was fourteen, at different times and in the mouths of different people, and there's no point now describing each of those circumstances because they're no different from what one would normally expect in such cases, and I would again have to speak of people who had left because they couldn't bear to witness what I did during those almost three decades, and it's amazing how you can build a career and write books and get married three times and wake up every morning despite what you have repeatedly done during those almost three decades, my third wife's plea was, of course, for me to stop drinking.

35.

In the long term drink slows down your reflexes, but that wasn't why my third wife made that plea. People who drink are prone to developing gastritis, stomach ulcers, hepatitis, heart problems and high blood pressure, chronic malnutrition, bipolar disorder, cirrhosis of the liver and generalised organ failure, but that wasn't why she said she would leave if I didn't listen to her. My third wife knew my history, and I could have said that I was ill and argued that I wasn't in control of my actions, and alleged that the reason I was still drinking was because of João and the memory of the last day I spoke to him, me sitting in my room with that bottle of whisky, the first and last time that I wept over what I would become from then on, a solitary, silent weeping, with no sense of pride or relief, I could have alleged whatever I liked, but that wasn't the problem: it wasn't simply a matter of choice or willpower, but the condition laid down by my third wife if I was to stay with her, knowing that staying would mean going ahead with the idea of us having a child.

THE DIARY

1.

It's impossible to read my father's memoir without seeing in it a reflection of my grand-father's notebooks. Both men decided to devote their final years to the same kind of project, and it would be absurd to suggest that this was pure coincidence, but in certain very spe-cific ways the tone they adopt is utterly different.

2.

Did my father have an objective in writing down his memories, sending me a message he had never managed to convey to me in forty years? Ever since I went to see him in Porto Alegre to give him the news about Alzhe-imer's I've been wondering if such a thing would even be possible after so much time, or after any amount of time, a few words or a whole book intended to change the way a son feels about his father, something a son knows from the moment he's born, the judgement he silently makes when he's still so fragile and

201

entirely dependent on his father's love, and there's no point in the father spending the rest of his years trying to redeem himself for being distant or indifferent or for deliberately or accidentally withholding his love, because that first memory is what will have lodged in the son's mind, whatever age he might be.

3.

From the age of fourteen on, my father never stopped feeling what he had always felt about my grandfather, and I imagine that the discovery of the notebooks did little to change that, because while my grandfather's memoir can be summed up in the phrase *the world as it should be*, which presupposes an opposite idea: *the world as it really is*, I'm sure my father knew this long before he read it, that for my grandfather the real world meant Auschwitz, and if Auschwitz is the greatest tragedy of the twentieth century, which makes it the greatest tragedy of all centuries, given that the twentieth century is considered the most tragic of all, because never have so many people been bombed, shot, hanged, impaled, drowned, butchered or electrocuted before being burned or buried alive, two million in Cambodia, twenty million in the Soviet Union, seventy million in China, hundreds of millions if one includes Angola, Algeria, Armenia, Bosnia, Bulgaria, Chechnya, Chile, the Congo, Cuba, Czechoslovakia, Egypt, El Salvador, Ethiopia, Haiti, Honduras, Hungary, India, Indonesia, Iran, Iraq, Korea, Lebanon, Libya, Mexico, Myanmar, Pakistan, Palestine, the Philippines, Poland, Portugal, Romania, Rwanda, Sierra Leone, Somalia, Spain, Sri Lanka, Sudan, Tibet, Turkey and Vietnam, an accumulation of corpses, a pile reaching up to the sky, the history of the world as nothing but an accumulation of massacres that lie behind every speech, every gesture, every memory, and if Auschwitz is the tragedy that contains in its essence all those other tragedies, it's also in a way proof of the non-viability of human experience at all times and in all places — in the face of which there is nothing one can do or think, no possible deviation from the path my grandfather followed during those years, the same period in which my father was born and grew up, unable ever to change that certain fate.

4.

The non-viability of human experience at all times and in all places was a concept freely available to my father. He had more right than anyone to grasp it in order to justify whatever attitude he chose to take during his life: he could have become the worst boss and the worst friend and the worst husband and the worst father because when he was fourteen he came face to face with that concept, with my grandfather slumped across the desk, and then there was the fight we had when I decided to change schools and the conversation we had by the barbecue, and the way he reacted to my going to university and my move to São Paulo, my three marriages and the day I told him he had Alzheimer's, all those things could have been very different, and I wouldn't be speaking about him now because I would have judged him already, and as was the case with him and my grandfather I would have nothing good to say about him, and as was the case with him and my grandfather I would feel no affection or empathy, and I would never have felt what a son naturally feels about his father without ever having to say or explain anything.

5.

I lived with my mother at the time. She didn't want to move just because of what happened to my father. I didn't even think about it then, nor did it occur to me that people would move when something like that happened. Because all his things were still there. Ten years later I would still sometimes find something of his. A napkin with his monogram on it. A pen. An ashtray.

6.

If I felt what my father had always felt about my grandfather, I wouldn't have gone to Porto Alegre when I found out he'd been diagnosed with Alzheimer's. I wouldn't have stopped my mother from falling as she stood swaying at the door to their apartment. I wouldn't have been welcomed by my father as if he already knew everything too, standing there immaculately combed and shaved, wearing a smart shirt and shoes, two o'clock in the afternoon and there he was ready to go out to lunch or to a meeting still smelling of the shaving lotion he'd put on, and all to receive the news that in less than five years he would be technically dead, and had I understood him as little as he did my grandfather, had I known nothing of the deep pool of grief that lay hidden until the fight we had when I was thirteen and he finally stopped using Nazism as an excuse for my grandfather, for what he really felt about my grandfather — something I only realised many years later and only properly grasped very recently, when I had access to my father's memoir — had my relationship with him been ruined in the way his relationship with my grandfather had, I wouldn't have flown to Porto Alegre to tell him that he had Alzheimer's and wouldn't have realised that this would change not only his life, but mine as well.

7.

There are two possible responses to the non-viability of human experience at all times and in all places. There is my grandfather's response, and I think I told my father everything I had to say on that subject when I was thirteen, in the only way I could at that age, and when I think about that fight today and the way my father looked at me during the fight and during our conversation on the day after the fight and the way he behaved subsequently, I realise that he secretly accepted I was right, and had known this for a long time, and that he could have come out with exactly the same words I had used, those I could muster at the time, and until then no one had so bluntly reminded my father that my grandfather had clung on to an excuse, made it his alibi, an aura that turned him into a kind of martyr, a saint, despite having ruined my father's life by following to the letter the predictions contained in the tons of books and thousands of films and endless hours of discussion about the non-viability of the human experience at all times and in all places and the inevitable fate met by all those who came in contact with it, even when that non-viability bore a name as symbolic and beyond debate as Auschwitz.

8.

Is it possible to hate an Auschwitz survivor in the way my father did? Is it permissible to feel such pure hatred, without at any moment falling into the temptation of moderating that feeling because of Auschwitz, without feeling guilty for placing one's own emotions above something like the memory of Auschwitz?

9.

Is it possible that one's hatred of an Auschwitz survivor could indicate a kind of indifference towards Auschwitz, as if hating the survivor, which can sometimes amount to wishing him ill, meant that you were indifferent to and might even endorse any evil done to him, even if that evil was carried out in Auschwitz?.

10.

The second possible response to the non-viability of human experience at all times and in all places is my father's. And if there is a way of summing up what a son feels for his father when he learns that his father is ill, I could simply mention that my father didn't do what my grandfather did, that he appears never even to have thought about it, and at no point did he give any indication that he had even so much as considered the idea that my birth made no difference, that my childhood meant nothing, that my presence could not keep him from succumbing in the way my grandfather succumbed. If I hadn't felt that gratitude towards him, which convinced me it was possible for a son to feel such a thing for his father, that it was possible for there to be something good about the relationship between son and father, reason enough still to believe in the relationship between son and father, were it not for that I wouldn't have told him that he had Alzheimer's, not after the ultimatum my third wife had just given me.

11.

I met my third wife at a dinner party. There were ten or fifteen of us sitting round a big table. The house belonged to an advertising executive. Advertising executives still enjoy buying and showing off paintings. I sat down opposite one of those images of polar bears that are supposed to suggest a kind of innocence but with a cosmopolitan touch, and I don't know whether it was our host's idea or simply the order in which the guests arrived, because I can't remember now if I got there early or late, if I was delayed by traffic or a meeting at the end of the day, or if my third wife was delayed because she couldn't decide what to wear or because of work or because one of her girlfriends rang her up at the last moment, I don't know if there was some special reason or if it was pure chance that she ended up sitting next to me.

12.

At the time I was drinking every night. I drank in the afternoons too, although not always and without it affecting my work too much. My work is perfectly compatible with heavy drinking, and not just because I get up late and work at home and only need two or three hours of concentrated work per day, enough to deliver two or three articles a week and publish two or three books every ten years, but also because at forty, alcohol still doesn't seriously affect you: contrary to what people think, you can continue to age without any of your organs showing any change in any of the tests you arrange to have done, each time scarcely able to believe that you've survived unscathed yet again.

13.

Before the age of forty, alcohol is more happy than sad. The nights of a drinker are better than those of a non-drinker. The conversations of a drinker are more amusing than those of a non-drinker. People who drink are more attractive than those who don't. The feeling of going home on a Wednesday morning when it's already light and looking at the non-drinkers making their way to an office where they'll spend nearly two-thirds of the day feeling proud of themselves because at least they're not like you, sitting in a local café drinking a glass of chocolate milk laced with brandy, the non-drinkers sitting in their cars and thinking you're just a forty-year-old idiot who hasn't yet realised he's not eighteen any more, and it's because you know that at the end of the day and the month you'll be exactly like all of them, having paid or not paid your rent, being employed or unemployed, having a marriage, health insurance, a vase of flowers, that, ultimately, it all comes down to the same thing even though you live each minute far more intensely than any of them, that's why you leave the café and walk unsteadily back to your apartment where you say hi to the caretaker and enter your apartment and feel no shame at all as you fall onto the bed with your shoes still on, until your third wife decides that enough is enough.

14.

My real problem with drink isn't physical exactly. It isn't material either, in the sense that you can compare the wealth and the work record of someone who drinks with someone who doesn't. As with everything in this story, it's a problem that goes back to when I was fourteen, when I changed schools for the second time and, grown weary of swimming against the tide, tried to fit in with the norm: my classmates in the third school also mixed *cachaça* with cola, they also borrowed the car of whoever's father happened to be away travelling so that we could visit bars and parties and crowded streets and find some excuse to end the night as we always did, someone else's girlfriend, someone's clothes, someone's appearance or the way someone moved or breathed, because all you have to do is hold your victim's gaze and make sure he's with friends in whose presence he can't be seen to be backing down, you just have to touch his shoulder, give him a tiny shove, poke him with your finger, so that in the ensuing fifteen minutes of every Friday and Saturday night, for years and years, you can continue to prove that you're not afraid of anything or anyone.

15.

I never took classes in boxing, capoeira or judo. I never did karate or jiu-jitsu. I spent years fighting in the most varied of places and for the most varied of reasons, and I never used any technique other than force mixed with a kind of courage that is almost a desire to get as badly beaten up as your opponent: a sprained wrist after delivering a punch, a cut to your forehead after headbutting someone, the day you have to be taken to hospital and spend the next week telling everyone you were attacked by three older assailants armed with nunchuks and butcher's knives, and until I received my third wife's ultimatum I would have been capable of offering the most varied of explanations as to why I'd always behaved like that, as if it were something involuntary, a genetic predisposition or a trauma resulting from everything I'd experienced from fourteen onwards, because that kind of reasoning allows you to justify anything, even the worst, the most grotesque of actions, the kind you only confess to at the very end of your argument.

16.

I could have continued taking that line of defence, and returned to the mantra that begins on the day when I stopped talking to João, as if that day were a rite of passage, the

213

discovery that everyone at some point needs to make, my grandfather standing before the gates of Auschwitz, my father standing before my grandfather sprawled across his desk, and the fact that at the time I thought of those three things as equivalents, Auschwitz for my grandfather and my grandfather's death for my father and the last note I received from João, Auschwitz and a suicide and a crumpled piece of paper from a notebook, Auschwitz and a suicide and a pencilled drawing, just the fact that I once thought of those three things as equivalents could also be seen as further proof of the non-viability of human experience at all times and in all places, and I could have spent the rest of my life using that statement as a justification for what I did to other people and to myself in the years that followed, the break-up of my first marriage after which I still couldn't behave in any other way, the break-up of my second marriage after which I still couldn't behave in any other way, my third wife with whom I tested the limits still further, and when I left that café it was like another test, me stumbling home and saying hi to the caretaker and entering the apartment and falling onto the bed with my shoes still on, and then my third wife waking up and confronting me and me looking at her and for the last time giving her my usual response.

17.

My third wife wakes up and asks where I
was before I fell onto the bed with my shoes
still on. She asks me to explain why on the
previous two mornings I had also fallen
onto the bed with my shoes still on. She's
tired of asking the same questions and
hearing the same answers and us spending
the whole night awake because she won't
resign herself to seeing me in that state, nor
to hearing my usual answer whenever she
brings the subject up, the fact that I don't
want to see what she sees, and don't want
to admit what is as clear as day to her, and
it's then that the tone of this telling-off
becomes accusatory, and the volume rises
and the anger grows until I can't stand the
hell of spending whole nights like this and I
aim a kick at the television, and my third
wife leaps up and flings herself on top of me
as if terrified that something really bad is
about to happen, and then I grab her by the
shoulders and shake her hard and, just as
I've been doing since I was fourteen years
old, I set to: I throw her down on the bed
(João, Auschwitz, my grandfather and my
father, the non-viability of human experience at all times and in all places) and
clench my fists (João, Auschwitz, my

215

grandfather and my father, the non-viability of human experience at all times and in all places) and look her in the face (João, Auschwitz, my grandfather and my father, the non-viability of human experience at all times and in all places) and then I do what I have to do.

18.

After ten years I got used to it. No one talked to me about it any more. No one took any notice when there was a report on TV about something similar. Over the years I had managed to concentrate on what interested me, the shop, my mother, and one of the things I learned over the years was never to show any weakness.

19.

My mother never knew that I would sometimes lock myself in my bedroom to cry. No one in the shop knew that I would sometimes, in the middle of the morning, lock myself in the toilet and stay there for ten minutes or half an hour crying.

20.

I cried at university. I cried in the car. In the street. I've cried at the cinema. In a restaurant. In a football stadium. At the swimming pool while I was swimming and afterwards in the changing room while I got dressed.

21.

After the fight I had with my father when I was thirteen, I was always drunk whenever I attacked someone physically. My third wife was the first to find this out and that was why the main condition she laid down when she issued her ultimatum was that I should stop drinking. This was the day after I kicked the television, during a relatively calm conversation we had, in which she told me that she wouldn't stay with me if I continued to behave like that, and that she would leave the apartment at once if she saw me in that state just one more time, and I would normally have let things end like that because that's what I'd always done until I was forty, and I was in no mood to deal with the situation, because it's painful to look at your wife, her nose, her right eye and her left eye, her mouth and teeth and her whole face which you could have struck and disfigured if, at the last moment, you hadn't diverted the blow and punched the mattress instead, missing her by about a centimetre.

22.

Punching the mattress meant that I didn't have to take her to the hospital or find myself being taken to the police station, but it didn't stop me falling limply onto the bed unable to say a word, filled by a torpor that was neither sadness nor guilt: there I was beside my third wife, thinking about what I'd been about to do to her, what I'd been doing to others and myself ever since I was fourteen years old, and I don't know what would have happened if the fight when I kicked the television hadn't occurred just before I found out that my father had Alzheimer's and I received my third wife's ultimatum, her calm voice saying that I wasn't fit to be the father of a child.

23.

It's impossible not to connect those two things: my trip to Porto Alegre and my third wife's calm voice pointing out to me the glaringly obvious. I talked to my father in his study, but my mother was always there too and her presence helped keep our minds off the subject, because my father was determined not to let her see how shaken he was, as if she were the one who needed to be consoled and treated with the slightly patronising air of adults trying to explain something difficult to a child, and all it took was for me to mention the word *Alzheimer's* for my father to take on that role and act as if the matter were of no immediate concern, and initially we discussed only whether he would need to have more tests done or get a second opinion, and that was when I realised that those steps would be taken one at a time.

24.

At first, my father treated the matter as if it were all merely part of the domestic routine, and I even had the impression that he insisted on my mother behaving as if nothing had happened, and made an effort in her presence to maintain his usual habits, and whenever I phoned my mother, she would say he was just the same, still grumbling, still making that annoying chewing noise and listening to the same radio programme every morning. It was as if she and I had convinced ourselves that my father was still the same person, as if each phone call were a kind of renewal of our licence to believe that. It became commonplace for him to repeat a question he had asked two minutes before, to overpay the cleaner or the caretaker, to change mood in the middle of a conversation, but the winter's afternoon when he would surprise my mother still seemed a long way off, an unfamiliar gesture, a word she had never heard him use in over forty years of marriage, a novelty that announced a still faster rate of change, my father losing a little of what we both thought of as unique to him, then one morning he wakes up and can't remember the name of a city, and the next whether a particular animal flies or swims or crawls, and the day after, the colour of his own car and how you use the accelerator and the brake, and suddenly he doesn't know how many years he's been married to my mother, and on that winter's afternoon, while she's drinking tea and listening distractedly to the wall clock striking five, she realises that he has no idea who he is or what he's doing there.

25.

How long will it be before that day arrives? The day when he can no longer feed himself. Or be able to take a bath without help. And no longer know when it's time to go to the toilet. And he'll need to be washed and dressed and sat in an armchair and put to bed and will spend the time muttering to himself. While no one can say with any certainty when that's going to happen, it may be that for my father the alarm bell has already sounded, and he knows that it's time to do what needs to be done and say what needs to be said, and I think that's why he sent me the first attachment containing his memoir.

26.

It was only the first part, twenty or thirty pages of what I imagine he will continue writing until he's filled, who knows, a hundred, two hundred pages? Or nine hundred, given that the last half will be incomprehensible? I don't know if that's what he intends to do, send me another batch every month or two for me to read and perhaps comment on, because he may want me to say something about it, to understand the message it contains, as he understood the message when he read my grandfather's note-books, if either of those memoirs can be said to contain a message.

27.

I cried in the street. In a hotel. On a bus. In a bookshop. In the supermarket. In the park. In a spare parts depot. In a lift. At a petrol station. On a viewing point from which you can see the whole city, but where no one could see me. In the shower, sitting in the tray, while the hot water collected all around me.

28.

I used to cry out of rage and shame, but I didn't want to waste any more time talking about it. I'd talked a lot already. Or perhaps I hadn't, but I think you understood. I wanted to consider the matter closed because it isn't really a subject that interests you greatly. I think you'd rather know more about that other night. The music being played. The musicians all wearing dinner jackets. The room neither very big nor very small, enough

I think to hold about one hundred and fifty people.

29.

Only Jews could be members of that particular club, but there were no Jewish symbols on the walls. I was wearing a tie, and it felt as if everyone in the room wanted to know if I was going to continue talking to her or turn my back. That was my main concern, what do I do now? She was sitting down. I had to bend my head a little so that she could hear me. I couldn't speak too loudly into her ear. Or too softly. Or stand too far away. Or too close.

30.

The band began to play the next tune, and I immediately asked her to dance. She got up and I didn't know whether to take her hand or to place my hand on her shoulder. I decided not to touch her at all. Only in the middle of the dance floor, where there were more people, did I place my hands on her waist. First one, then the other. I went to the middle of the room because that seemed the polite thing to do. Then she wouldn't think I was trying to lead her into some dark corner. That was the first time I felt her body. I leaned closer, and we stayed there, moving in circles round the dance floor. I think that lasted about two minutes. The two of us there. I closed my eyes and preferred not to say anything. The next tune started up. Then the next. I spent four or five dances pressed close to her and saying nothing. I think that was the right thing to do and she must have liked it. That was better than pretending to be someone I wasn't. I was so full of anger about so many things, so full of shame, but, as I said before, I don't want to talk about that any more. There comes a point when you get tired of even thinking about it. No one's life can be taken up by that alone. Look at my life now, look at what's happening to me. Is it worth going over and over it? Is it worth suffering because of it? Could I really cry about it all these years later? I prefer to remember other things, me in the middle of the dance floor with her. I wasn't nervous any more. The worst was over. I think the whole story began there. At least the story that's worth telling. The one I want to talk about in this letter, or this book, however you want to call it. Everything I have to say begins there, with me in a dance hall holding your mother in my arms and saying nothing.

31.

My grandfather's memoir can be summed up in the phrase *how the world should be*, and you could almost say that my father's memoir is along the lines of *how things really were*, and since both are, in a way, complementary texts on the same theme, the non-viability of human experience at all times and in all places, with my grandfather immobilised by that and my father managing to move on despite it, and since it's impossible to talk about the two without taking up a position on the subject, the fact is that, right from the start, this text has been a justification for that position.

32.

A father can't attack his wife in front of their child. He can't run the risk of attacking her. He can't even think about doing anything that might make him run that risk, a glass, a sip, a drop of drink from a bottle locked in a cupboard inside a room with an iron bolt on the door, even the smell of drink within a radius of a few kilometres around the house and the street and the school and anywhere else frequented by your child until he's strong enough to suspect that something like that might happen in some family somewhere in the world. I don't know how things would have turned out if I hadn't convinced myself of that on the journey to and from Porto Alegre, my third wife's ultimatum getting mixed up with what happened on that journey, but what other subject has had more written about it than a son faced by his dying father?

33.

I wouldn't want to tell another of those stories about how being in an extreme situation forces us to re-evaluate our whole life, as if the prospect of someone close to us dying made us realise how unimportant everything else is. I wouldn't want to use that journey to Porto Alegre, the conversations I had with my father after I'd told him about the illness, while I accompanied him when he went to have further tests, and spent the afternoons with him and cooked with him, and made sure he wasn't left too much alone, two weeks in Porto Alegre and it was just as it used to be when I was fourteen, and we were on the beach or sitting by the barbecue, and he again asked me about my life, and it became natural again for me to confide in him, and describe to him my third wife's ultimatum, to tell him about the drinking and the fighting and the aggression, my closest kept secret, all the things I was capable of feeling with my father there, precisely because he was there, the places and people who were dying at the very moment I discovered that I was still capable of feeling those things, the last significant conversation we had before that evolving illness made such confessions pointless, and I wouldn't want to attribute to those days and to that conversation my decision to have a child, but looking back that's pretty much how things happened.

34.

The non-viability of human experience at all times and in all places has the advantage of making things less painful and more amusing. It's easy enough to scoff at the idea that some-one might have decided to make his father and himself a kind of present, for both of them to live those final years differently, a father seeing his son give up drinking, give up destroying him-self and others, give up his determination to die without having understood anything. Per-haps my father would be there at every stage, my third wife's pregnancy, the first positive test, the first visit to the doctor, the first medical checks, the first time you could hear the baby's heartbeat, me telling my father what sex the child was and about my third wife's health and the last weeks before the birth, her difficulties sleeping, the pains in her legs, her breathlessness, and those days in Porto Alegre were enough for me to see that there could be time for all those things, my father alive and conscious when the waters broke and the contractions began and my wife and I set off together to the hospital, my father holding his grandson afterwards, one man and his farewell and one man and his re-beginning, the last time my father will say my name and the first time I will say yours.

35.

My third wife has just found out she's pregnant, and that's why I've said so little about her, her name, her profession, her likes and dislikes.

36.

You'll have your whole life to get to know her, and that's why I've said little or nothing about what she means to me, something I've known ever since the dinner party where we first met.

37.

We didn't talk much to begin with. Someone at the table made a disparaging remark about the painting with the polar bears, and I laughed, and maybe she liked my laugh, the sound I make, my shoulders shaking or not and my own remark on the innocent but cosmopolitan tastes of our advertising executive host, a joke that might have been deemed inoffensive or entirely inappropriate in the circumstances, and I don't know at what point I mentioned that I had recently separated from my wife, if I did so spontaneously or in response to someone else who brought the subject up, or if I did so in a tone of voice that didn't sound too coarse or indifferent or self-congratulatory given the situation, which called for or should call for a degree of restraint or regret, but she clearly approved of my behaviour to some degree because we immediately introduced ourselves and started talking, and from then on chance had nothing to do with it.

38.

For my part, I couldn't explain it either: if it was something she said during that first conversation, if it was her perfume, her clothes, her hair, her hands, the way she held her fork, the way she wiped her mouth before picking up her glass, the way she allowed me to press my knee against hers and how at one point in the evening she looked at me to indicate that she knew I could feel the warmth of her leg, and for a fraction of a second both she and I held our ground instead of averting our gaze or making some ironic, distancing gesture as if that contact were purely accidental, just a fraction of a second, and the person you had been up until then becomes the past, something suddenly clicks, and the supper and the conversation and the days and years that follow become something else, and it was all so quick and delicate and yet unmistakable because in four decades you had never before experienced such a sense of things to come.

39.

If it hadn't been for that, I wouldn't have invited your mother out on a date a few days after that supper. Or courted your mother. Or lived with her under the same roof. Or made an effort to persuade her to take me back each time the non-viability of human experience at all times and in all places showed its face in fights like the one when I kicked the television, Auschwitz and a suicide and me almost attacking the one person I'd fallen in love with, Auschwitz and a suicide and me nearly turning my back on the one person I'd fallen in love with, Auschwitz and João and my grandfather and my father and me nearly throwing away what that person was offering me, the sheer luck, the miracle of having met her, and when I say *miracle* I consider it an equal miracle that despite everything she didn't simply leave me, that despite everything she's pregnant, and that despite everything the whole circle will, very shortly, be complete.

40.

Having a son means leaving behind you the non-viability of the human experience at all times and in all places, as if it no longer made any sense to talk about the ways in which it manifests itself in all our lives, and the various ways in which we each try and succeed in freeing ourselves from it. In my case everything can be reduced down to the day when I stopped drinking, when I began politely refusing any drinks, when I began politely saying that I don't drink, not even a glass of wine or a cocktail in the company of friendly, well-intentioned people, because it wouldn't be good for me, and it's easier than it seems and I'm not trying to promote abstinence, the reason I'm saying what I think about it now is so that in the future you'll be able to read this and reach your own conclusions. Because I'm not going to spoil your childhood by going on about it. I'm not going to ruin your life by making everything revolve around that. You'll be starting from zero and you don't want to have to carry the weight of all that or anything else other than what you'll discover for yourself, the house where you're going to live, the cradle you're going to sleep in, the first time you feel hunger, thirst, cold, tiredness, loneliness, the gratuitous pain caused by colic or infection, the sense of abandonment one day when everyone's sleeping, the fear of the dark when you start choking and there's no one around, the reflux, the sob, the bad dream that never ends, the rumble of thunder, a sound you don't know and can't tell where it comes from, the helplessness, agony, horror and despair which, at that moment, are

232

your one reality, but then someone takes care of all those things and normality is restored when you're fed and given some medicine and have your nappy changed and they put you in the bath, and the water is warm, and there's the little duck, the bubbles, the toy trumpet, the mirror, the fluffy towel, your mother's arms and skin, her smell, the touch of her hands as she sits you on my lap, the clothes I put on you, my beard, the sound of my voice, the words I'll say and which are still incomprehensible, but you look at me and know intuitively what lies behind each and every one of them, what the person there means to you, like my grandfather and my father, my father and me, me here now and the feeling that will accompany you as the years pass, as I begin to forget all the rest, which at this point is neither happy nor sad, good or bad, true or false, part of a past that is likewise of no importance compared to what I am and will be, forty years old, with everything still before me, from the day that you're born.

We do hope that you have enjoyed reading this large print book.

Did you know that all of our titles are available for purchase?

We publish a wide range of high quality large print books including:
Romances, Mysteries, Classics
General Fiction
Non Fiction and Westerns

Special interest titles available in large print are:
The Little Oxford Dictionary
Music Book
Song Book
Hymn Book
Service Book

Also available from us courtesy of Oxford University Press:
Young Readers' Dictionary
(large print edition)
Young Readers' Thesaurus
(large print edition)

For further information or a free brochure, please contact us at:
Ulverscroft Large Print Books Ltd.,
The Green, Bradgate Road, Anstey,
Leicester, LE7 7FU, England.
Tel: (00 44) 0116 236 4325
Fax: (00 44) 0116 234 0205

Other titles published by Ulverscroft:

A MAP OF NOWHERE

Martin Bannister

David Price always wished life would blow up in his face. And then it did. His mother died; the urge to paint left him; and Sarah came his way — followed by Pete, a psychiatric outpatient. Now David spends his time worrying about Sarah's eating habits, visiting her terminally ill sister, and working as Pete's carer. But when Pete's odd behaviour starts to leave David fearing for his own safety, he is shocked to discover that Sarah knows the reason why — but will not disclose it . . .

2 A.M. AT THE CAT'S PAJAMAS

Marie-Helene Bertino

Madeleine is two days away from being ten. She needs a haircut, is unofficially forbidden from singing in church or school assembly, and smokes Newport Menthols from the carton her mother was smoking when she died at the beginning of the year. Her mother had filled a recipe box with instructions on how to do various things she knew she wouldn't be around to teach her daughter: how to make a fist; how to change a flat tire; how to write a thank-you note for a gift you hate. And one card, she listed the rules of singing. The #1 rule: KNOW YOURSELF . . .

THE WATER IS WIDE

Liz Gilbey

Artist Mikki Webster takes her beloved narrow-boat, *Serendipity*, on a holiday tour of Britain's waterways, stopping in at Bleakhall to visit her brother Jonny and his wife Tracy. The couple have their hands full — renovating their canal-side cottage, launching their new careers, and coping with an imminent baby as well as their rebellious teenager Katie. When Katie has a serious motorbike accident, Mikki stays moored beside Wharf Cottage in order to lend a hand. But sparks fly when Mikki, working at the boatyard, encounters Bill Rankin — the pop star she had fallen in love with all those years ago . . .

BEYOND REASON

Gwen Kirkwood

Young Janet Scott loves books and learning, and is happy living at the schoolhouse wher her grandfather is the dominie. Her world is shattered when he dies and the new schoolmaster's petty cruelty becomes intolerable. Sent to work for farmer Wull Foster, Janet becomes the target of his dangerous lechery, and escapes. Taken in by the kind philanthropist Josiah Saunders, an old friend of her grandfather's, she is pitched into a dilemma when he offers her the security of an amiable but passionless marriage. For her heart belongs to another: her childhood friend, the penniless lawyer's clerk Fingal McLauchlan . . .

APHRODITE'S ISLAND

Hilary Green

1955: The island of Cyprus is torn apart by EOKA's insurrection against British rule. Seventeen-year-old Ariadne's family are deeply involved in the rebellion, guarding hidden caches of rifles to arm the militants. But when British soldier Stephen Allenby arrives to search their house, a spark ignites between him and Ariadne: despite their divided loyalties, the two fall in love . . . 1973: Back in England, Stephen labours under the twin shadows of a strained marriage and miserable job. Then the rise of EOKA-B sends him back to Cyprus as a foreign correspondent and information-gatherer, all the while searching the island for the memories of his youth . . .

THE LIVING

Léan Cullinan

The Troubles may be officially over but, for the first generation to come of age in Ireland's flimsy peacetime, the ghosts of the past are all too close to home . . . Cate Houlihan is adrift in a life that doesn't feel her own, struggling with a new job at an eccentric publishing house and stifled by overbearing parents. When romance blossoms with the gorgeous, intelligent — and British — Matthew Taylor, it seems as if things might finally be going her way. But Cate's job brings her into contact with the country's Republican past. And the lines between this, her family, and her new relationship are beginning to blur . . .